In My Dreams
I Walk with You

Dennis Walters with James Achenbach

Sleeping Bear Press
310 North Main Street
P.O. Box 20
Chelsea, MI 48118
www.sleepingbearpress.com

Printed and bound in the United States

10 9 8 7 6 5 4 3 2 1

Library of Congress Cataloging-in-Publication Data on File
ISBN: 1-886947-87-2

*This book is dedicated to my family—my wonderful and always
supportive sister, Barbara; my niece, Brodie; and to the
memory of my mom and dad, Florence and Bucky Walters,
for without these people there would be no book.*

– *Foreword* –

I first heard of Dennis Walters in 1974 when my friend Mickey Van Gerbig told me about Dennis's tragic accident. Mickey knew Dennis well and he told me that he had been a fine young player who loved golf very much. I remember thinking that it was a shame that because he was now paralyzed from the waist down he would never be able to play this great game again. Boy, was I ever wrong. Not only has Dennis come back to play golf again, he has had a wonderful career as one of the game's finest trick-shot artists and performers.

Back in 1974, the odds of Dennis succeeding in the remarkable way that he has were probably impossible to calculate. How many practice shots must he have hit? How much time and effort must he have put into perfecting his skills and inventing new ways of hitting a golf ball? Whatever it took, though, Dennis did it. And believe me, if you ever see his show you will be amazed at his ball-striking ability. His consistency is even more remarkable considering the fact that he uses some of the strangest golf equipment that I have ever seen—clubs with multiple heads, clubs with hinges, and clubs with hoses for shafts. What Dennis can do with a golf club is beyond imagination; it simply has to be seen to be believed.

Dennis's show, however, is about much more than hitting perfect golf shots. As he puts it, "The experience is not only about golf lessons but life lessons, too." And what Dennis is really demonstrating is that with hard work, perseverance, and sheer determination, dreams can come true. This is a message that should be heard by as many people as possible—golfer and nongolfer, young and old, those both physically fit and physically challenged—and Dennis has been working hard to spread the word. And while it is true that his amazing accomplishments will never make golf's record book, it is equally true that he has touched and inspired hundreds of thousands of people all over the world.

I am certain that you will appreciate Dennis's story as much as I did. At times you will cry and at times you will laugh. But by the time you finish the last page, you may be inspired to chase your own dream that you once thought was unreachable. He inspires us all to live life to its fullest. My friend, Dennis Walters, does just that.

Jack Nicklaus
North Palm Beach, Florida

– Contents –

Chapter 1

The Last Shot

ON THE LAST HOLE of the last round of my competitive career—a pro-am tournament at Bonnie Briar Country Club in Larchmont, New York—my golf ball was buried in a greenside bunker. I had not played well but I had fought hard all day. I was 24 years old and would soon play in the PGA Qualifying Tournament (now known as "Q School").

The final green was elevated five feet above me. Since I had missed my approach on the short side of the green, I only had a few feet of area on which to stop my ball—a miracle shot from a tough, buried lie. Little did I know that this would be the last full shot I would hit using my legs. I looked up once more and knew that it would be a difficult shot because the ball was so deep in the sand that I could barely see it. Yet it was a shot I had practiced literally hundreds of times since I first began to play the game. I slowly twisted my feet in the sand, feeling solid, feeling ready. It felt good. I made an aggressive swing with my trusty old brown-shafted sand wedge, and sand went flying everywhere. My senses were so acute at that moment that it seemed as if the ball were floating in slow motion toward the pin. It hit the green, rolled ever so slightly, and stopped within a few inches of the hole. I had just hit the greatest bunker shot of my life. The ball was so close to the hole, I was able to tap it in with my wedge. It turned out to be the last shot I ever hit standing under my own power.

That shot is perhaps more vivid than any other of my golf memories. It was July 21, 1974, the final day that I would ever walk on this sweet earth without assistance. I was so proud of myself right then. I had played terribly (I think I shot 77) but I tried on every shot, especially the last one. Maybe that's why I can almost still "feel" the shot more than 27 years later.

My friend Bob Watson—the head pro at the time at Wykagyl Country Club in New Rochelle, New York—got to witness my early development as a golf professional. Today, it seems appropriate that Bob was the person responsible for my becoming his assistant. He was a pro's pro, and many people considered him one of America's best club professionals. Even at age 75, long retired from his prestigious jobs at such well-known clubs as Wykagyl and Westchester Country Club, he still could play the game with such authority that he managed to qualify for the British Senior Open.

Back then, Bob Watson was looking for young golf professionals who lived and breathed the game, and I surely fit the bill. He hired me as an assistant pro at Wykagyl early in 1974. At that time, I essentially had no other interests except golf. I lived above the locker room at the club in what you might call a 'crow's nest.' I ate at the club, taught at the club, and played golf at the club. As you can tell, golf was my life.

When I went to work for Bob, two of the things he told me was that I would not have to work in the pro shop and that I would be playing in pro-ams and other tournaments. It was such a great job that it did not even seem like one. I played with anybody who wanted to play golf—kids, adults, members, guests, anyone. That was my job and that was it. The rest of the time I practiced.

On the morning of my last day as a walking golf pro, I sat in the Wykagyl kitchen and ate bacon and eggs prepared by the club's chef. It is the golfer's great breakfast, and I was getting ready for a full day of golf.

Something else I remember about that pro-am at Bonnie Briar, in addition to that last shot, was that I had topped a tee shot with a 3-wood. I had very rarely done that, so I knew I needed to do some work on my game—especially after having played such a poor round of golf. It was late July and Tour qualifying in September was not too far away. I had reason to be concerned. I knew I needed to be ready, and I was determined to be.

I had plans to spend that night and the next day with my buddy, Ralph Terry, the former New York Yankee pitching ace who was also a golf professional. It never ceased to amaze me that every time I saw Ralph I always left feeling better, both about my golf game and about myself. I think it was because he never let anything bother him. He always had a positive attitude and I hoped that it would rub off on me. The best thing about Ralph was that he really knew my game and could pick out the things I needed to work on. Like me, he could practice all day long and never get tired of it. We would go out to the course, hit balls, practice our putting and play. From the first time I met Ralph, when he was winding down his baseball career with the New York Mets and I was a 16-year-old kid, I knew we would be great friends.

During the 12 years that Ralph pitched in the major leagues, he held at least two distinctions. The first distinction was that, on two occasions, he threw the last pitch in the seventh game of a World Series. The first time he did it, unfortunately, came in the 1960 World Series. Pitching for the New York Yankees, Ralph gave up the famous seventh-game, ninth-inning home run to Bill Mazeroski of the Pittsburgh Pirates. Two years later he bounced back in heroic fashion, being named Most Valuable Player in the World Series after beating the San Francisco Giants 1-0 in the seventh game. Near the end of his baseball career, Ralph achieved his second distinction. He was an active baseball professional *and* a golf professional at the same time. He spent two additional seasons with the Yankees, was traded to Cleveland before the 1965 campaign, and then finished his career as a New York Met before being released by the team in 1967. It was then that he became the full-time golf professional at Roxiticus Golf Club, a private facility where he was one of the investors.

When I spent time with Ralph, I always felt like I was part of his family. I enjoyed being with his wife, Tanya, and his sons, Gabe and Raif, with whom I hit it off perfectly. So, as usual, one of the reasons I was looking forward to spending time with Ralph was because he always made me feel good mentally when I was around him. A lot of times I was hard on myself and I would get depressed about my game and sometimes about life in general. I could not wait to see him that day. I knew he would pick up my spirits and everything would be better.

– Chapter 2 –

The Accident

AS IT TURNED OUT, everything would not be better. In fact, every-thing became crazy, chaotic, unthinkable, and unknown. Even so, it never erased my desire to overcome my difficulties. More than a quarter century later, I have a message that I constantly deliver to those who attend my golf shows. And I say it to one and all, whether they have golf experience or not. "Never give up," I tell them. "Never, *ever* give up." Fortunately, this was something I had always believed. I had also been taught that if you want something bad enough, if you make the effort, then you will have a chance to achieve your goal. Winners never quit trying.

On Sunday, July 21, 1974, this philosophy was about to be tested to its core. I finished the tournament at Bonnie Briar and then drove to Mendham, New Jersey, to see Ralph at his club. That's where the accident happened—10 minutes down the road from the United States Golf Association headquarters in Far Hills, New Jersey.

When I arrived at Roxiticus, a place where I had been count-less times before, I went in to the golf shop and asked if anybody knew where Ralph was. I was told that he was playing the back nine so I practiced my putting and chipping on the putting green. After a while, I guess I got impatient and decided to grab a cart to go out and look for him.

I started my search by heading down the 10th fairway, but did not find him. At one point in my search for Ralph I was driving downhill on a cart path that was intended to take golfers *uphill*. Over and over, I have replayed that day in my mind. *Should* I— *could* I—have done it differently? Was there some way to sidestep fate? If only I had taken a different route to look for Ralph.

The questions were endless. They still are. How many thousands of times had I driven a golf cart? How many thousands of times had I, like many golfers, driven one so casually or even carelessly? On this day, however, I wasn't careless. I maneuvered the cart down the hill with patience. I was aware of everything around me. The blue stones on the cart path, the stones that would be my undoing, did not go unnoticed.

I was in an old three-wheel golf cart, a style that's not made anymore because it proved to be unstable. Up ahead was a fork. If you angled to the left, you'd go to the 12th tee. If you angled to the right, you'd go down to the 16th green—and the path there was very steep. After thinking at first about going to the left, I finally decided to go to the right. To this day, I'm not quite sure why. It was probably because I was figuring that Ralph was either on the 15th hole or the 16th hole. As I said, the path I took headed downhill—steeply. At the bottom there was another right-hand turn, a sharp one. After you got around that turn, you went a little farther and there was the 16th green. Once I started down the hill, I was aware of the little blue stones on the cart path. I wasn't going that fast, but as I got to the turn the cart began to slide on the stones.

I think what happened was that the cart got going a little sideways. On both sides of the path were big rocks and washouts, so I probably tried to straighten the cart to avoid hitting something. The next thing I knew, though, the cart was starting to tip over. I've thought about that moment eight million times and I still don't actually know what happened. The only thing I remember about it was that the cart started to slide and then tip and it seemed as if I were frozen in time.

Adrenaline was surging through my entire body while this was happening and I actually saw my golf clubs flying through the air. It was like they were moving in slow motion. They were the tools of my trade and I had handpicked each one of them. I had a good-sized Hogan golf bag and in it was my set of Haig Ultra irons that I had gotten from a local salesman. Man, those irons were perfect, absolutely perfect. Originally I had wanted a different set. But then I noticed that a few guys on the PGA Tour had Haig Ultras so I got a set, too. Also in the bag was my "Rising Sun" Toney Penna MacGregor driver. To me, it was the best driver of all time. My RLB sand wedge (the initials of the original owner) was in there as well. Boy, did I love those clubs.

So anyhow, the next thing I know I'm lying on the ground and my clubs are scattered all over the place. I remember thinking: *I've got to get up because I've got to get my clubs.* My next thought was: *What the hell happened?* So I tried to get up but I couldn't move. I was lying flat on my back without a single cut or scratch on my body. My pants weren't even ripped. There wasn't any blood and I didn't feel any pain. In fact, everything seemed normal except that I couldn't move my legs. In an effort to get something going, out of fear probably, I started beating on my legs. But there was nothing, no feeling at all. The next thing I knew, several people, including Ralph, were running up to me and asking if I was OK. I don't think I ever lost consciousness.

I remember saying to somebody, "What's this all about?" Then I said, "Ralph, nothing hurts but I think I'm hurt pretty bad because I can't move my legs." He tried to reassure me. "I was in a car wreck one time and broke my hip," he said. "At first, I couldn't move my legs. But it went away, so don't worry about it." Somebody rushed back to the clubhouse to get a doctor and they actually found one on the tennis courts. When he got to me, the first thing he did was poke my legs with a sharp pin. "Do you feel this?" he asked. "Do you feel that?" I didn't feel a thing.

The next thing I remember was an ambulance pulling up. The Mendham Rescue Squad, a team that had received numerous awards for their work, arrived on the scene and somehow managed to back their vehicle down that steep hill to reach me. Thinking about it now, it's miraculous that they were able to do it. They were fantastic. As for me, I was bewildered because I didn't understand what was happening. I couldn't move my legs, but I wasn't in any pain. So it was confusing. Anyhow, after they got me in the ambulance, it took about 20 minutes to reach the emergency room at Morristown Memorial Hospital. Other than being taken to an operating room on a stretcher, I don't remember anything about the first hour or so after I got to the hospital. My parents and my sister Barbara weren't even there yet because they were stuck in traffic on the Garden State Parkway.

Up to that point, I had never been admitted to a hospital. Possibly I had visited friends or relatives who were patients, but I had no clear memory of it. Certainly no one in my family had ever been admitted to a hospital. So, at age 24 and healthy, a hospital was a very frightening and foreign place to me. Except for needing some stitches when I was four years old, I had never been injured. I also never got sick. I never had my tonsils or appendix removed , nothing. I had always been healthy. Now I was lying in a hospital, and I might as well have been on Mars.

Even with all of the activity going on all around me at the time, all I could think about was when I would play golf again. On the way to the operating room, I remember telling a staff member, "Fix me up, because I'm going to play on the PGA Tour." The rest is a blank. I woke up after the surgery and one of the nurses came by to give me something to drink and I immediately got sick to my stomach. That was just one of many indicators that left me confused and clueless about my condition following my surgery. One of the first things I heard somebody in recovery ask was, "If you can't stand up, how can you play golf?" But the thing that kept me going was the thought that I was going to get better. I was sure that I was going to regain the feeling in my legs and I would be able to walk again. I think the doctors were certain almost from the beginning that that was never going to happen, but nobody explained it to me for a long, long time.

Later on, I was told what had actually happened. When the cart tipped and I fell out, I dislocated a vertebra at thoracic level 12, or "T-12" as it is commonly referred to. Oddly enough, if I had *fractured* that same vertebra I would have been better off. But by being dislocated, it pinched a part of my spinal cord and that's what caused the paralysis. When I was thrown from the cart, I think I must have landed on one of those big rocks or on the corner of one of the washouts. Whatever I hit, the force on my body was enough to move the vertebra and pinch my spinal cord. It might have moved only a centimeter but the damage to my spinal cord was enough to intercept messages from my brain to certain parts of my body. The higher the vertebra, the more your body can be affected. My injury was at the base of my spinal cord, the area that controls inner body functions such as bowels, bladder, legs, and feet. I no longer could control those parts of my body.

As I slowly and reluctantly began to grasp the reality of what had happened to me, I became angrier and angrier. It was like there was this great volcano building up in my body, waiting to explode. I was like that for a long time.

Have I ever been back to Roxiticus Golf Club, where I had my accident? Hell, no. I will *never* go back there. Even if it were possible to put me in a foursome with Sam Snead, Ben Hogan, and Bobby Jones, I would not go back to that place.

No way in hell.

* * *

Today, my friend Ralph Terry is retired and living in his hometown of Larned, Kansas. He will tell you that he remembers the events of July 21, 1974 vividly. "As if it were yesterday," he says.

"I was playing with the president of the club and another member and one of their kids. Somewhere around the 14th or 15th holes, this member—not the president, the other man—had to leave early.

I found out later that he saw Dennis in the pro shop and he told him where we were on the course. The accident happened while we were on the 16th green.

"The course is set on two levels, with the 12th taking you down into the valley. The 16th finishes in a low area, too, but the 17th tee is on the upper level. The path that Dennis took was a winding one. Even though it was only occasionally used to go down, they had to make it wind like that to keep carts from going too fast. It was about 100 yards downhill from the top level to the bottom level and very steep. It had new stones on it and I am sure that they had not settled in just yet.

"We were just leaving the 16th green and our forecaddie was already headed up the hill. He came running back down and said there was somebody lying by the path and that a cart was overturned at the bottom. He said, 'Come back quick, I think it's Dennis.' He would have had to have put his brakes on and I think the cart started to skid. He was turning to the right and all the weight (both Dennis and his golf bag) was on the left side. I'm sure the cart tumbled over on him from the right side. The cart that Dennis was driving was an old Cushman with three wheels. The cart had some bars on it that apparently hit him in the back. The impact had a shearing effect on his spinal cord. When I looked around, the cart was all the way down the hill another 50-60 yards and was in the woods.

"When I finally got up to Dennis, he was gasping for air and was just lying there. I vividly remember Dennis's first words. 'Ralph, it's serious. I can't move my legs.' Well, I had been in an accident and had temporary loss of feeling in my legs, so I tried to comfort him that way. I sent somebody back to the clubhouse to call 911. They also found Dr. Kim playing tennis. He rushed out to the scene and brought some kind of pin with him. He scratched Dennis's stomach a couple of times in different places to see if he had any feeling and Dennis said yes. He then stuck him about four inches below the navel, but didn't tell Dennis. There was no reaction from Dennis. Dr. Kim turned to me and matter-of-factly said, 'He's going to be a paraplegic.' Neither one of us wanted Dennis to know at that point.

"The Mendham Rescue squad came and it was amazing what they did. They carefully backed down part of that hill, but did not go all the way down. They never let any part of Dennis's body move when they put him on the special stretcher that immobilizes a person. There were a couple of rocks under Dennis's back when they lifted him up. He had a lump—it had already become swollen—a big lump, bigger than your fist. The rescue people were just fabulous. I rode in the ambulance with him, and when we got to Morristown Memorial, his family had not yet arrived. Morristown Memorial is one of the great hospitals in the country and they had an orthopedic surgeon and a neurosurgeon waiting to examine Dennis. After their initial evaluation, one of the doctors, who didn't have much tact, bluntly told me, 'You can believe in miracles all you want, but this young man's life is changed. But I do need to get in there and clean things up in his back or he could lose his life.

"So they prepared to take him into surgery. Fortunately, his family finally got there after being stuck in traffic. It was a big boost to Dennis because they all gave him wonderful words of encouragement. After his surgery, Dennis began to realize that he might never walk again. That was really hard. He's part of our family and I can honestly look back and say that it was about the most tragic thing that ever happened to us. My wife, Tanya, and I have two boys. Dennis was like one of our kids. We had our little gang, you know, and we really had a lot of fun. He was as dedicated to the game of golf as anyone I had ever met. He was gifted. You just can't imagine how far he could hit the ball for someone his size. I had known him for almost 10 years at the time and I knew he had it in him to make it out on the PGA Tour.

"That moment in time (the accident), even though it was just a matter of a few minutes, seemed like an eternity to me after we had just spent a wonderful few days the month before at Winged Foot Golf Club in Mamaroneck, New York, to watch the U.S. Open. We walked all around the course and really had a good time.

Between that visit to the U.S. Open and his accident, Dennis had lost the New Jersey Open in a play-off with Art Silverstrone and Pat Schwab. Dennis shot 69 in the playoff and got beat by Silverstrone. I'll never forget Art's words as he talked about being older than Dennis. He said he didn't have many years left to win tournaments like this, but Dennis would have lots of opportunities to win. It sticks in my mind so clearly. Pretty ironic, huh? Who would have known what was going to happen just a short while later.

"I had first met Dennis when we were paired together in the 1965 New Jersey Open at Plainfield Country Club. It's an old Donald Ross course and I think Dennis was about 16 years old. He played with a whippy-shafted Power Bilt driver and was knocking it by me by about 20 yards.

"His game was just beautiful. I really loved the way he swung the club and hit the ball. He was bright, enthusiastic, and cheerful. He was just a young guy, and he was all golf. I liked that. We stayed in touch, and I would see him at other tournaments around the state. He would stop by Roxiticus or we would meet at different courses and play. I was familiar with his swing and how he hit the ball and how he approached golf.

"Even though he was just a kid, I had a lot of confidence in his ability. He was different. He always made it sound like music. It reminded me of watching the great hitters in baseball—Aaron, Musial, Williams, Mantle, and Mays. When they hit a ball, it had a different ring to it. It had that real pure sound. When you stood around the batting cage when those great hitters hit the ball, it was just more pure than anybody else.

"Dennis had a very logical mind for the golf swing. He really had the right attitude. He was stubborn in what he believed in. He believed there were certain ways to hit the ball, and he did not compromise his beliefs in the golf swing. Evan 'Big Cat' Williams (former World Long Drive champion) used to say that pound for pound, Dennis hit the ball farther than anybody he ever saw. Dennis was just a little guy (145 pounds), but he was all muscle.

"At Roxiticus, we did not have a driving range. There were very few members, so we would always practice on the 18th hole. We were hitting 6-irons one day, and I just wanted to see what kind of club head speed Dennis could generate. So I said to him, 'Let's see you really accelerate through this one,' never dreaming that he could hit it like he did. He hit that thing, and it must have flown about 220 yards and one-hopped into the clubhouse ballroom. It hit a window and made a little hole. Then it went rolling around on the hardwood floor where there was a table full of women playing bridge.

"I never feel sorry for myself for very long. I think about Dennis. He's an inspiration to me. I know that early on he contemplated suicide. I told him that there were other things in life to focus on. But he was *so* focused on golf. It doesn't amaze me that he has accomplished everything he has since the accident. He keeps my attitude in perspective. I used to mention that my knees were really bothering me. Dennis would laugh and say, 'Tell me about it.' He still has his sense of humor. We love him as a part of our family and there is not a day that goes by that we do not think about him."

– Chapter 3 –

Growing Up with Golf

MY FIRST MEMORY of playing golf was when I was about eight years old. We used to live about a mile or so from a wonderful public course called Jumping Brook Country Club. Everyone at the Jersey Shore, however, knew it as The Brook. It had rolling terrain, lots of trees, and was definitely not an easy course to score on. It came as no surprise that the course's layout was so challenging. Willard Wilkinson, a relative unknown in the world of golf architecture, designed it. His claim to fame, however, comes from the fact that he was an associate of A.W. Tillinghast, one of the most highly regarded architects of the twentieth century. Unfortunately, Jumping Brook was always in a ratty, rundown condition. The greens were unpredictable and the fairways were filled with clover and dandelions, which may have taught me at an early age to contend with different types of shots. I certainly do not regret learning to play golf there, and I consider the time that I spent to have been very valuable to my golf education. It was a wonderful place for a kid to hang out and learn the game. In fact what made it even more interesting was that, according to *Ripley's Believe It or Not,* "The Brook" was the only course where you could stand at the clubhouse and see all 18 greens and tees.

My dad played there a couple of times a week and usually scored in the low 80s. On his best day, he could break 80. Dad bought an annual family membership for $500 so that he could play there with his buddies on the weekends. My earliest recollection is going to the huge swimming pool at The Brook and spending the day while my dad played golf. The pool was on a hill and overlooked a large putting green. When I got tired of swimming, I remember wandering over to the putting green. I recall standing on the green, barefooted and thinking how good the closely mowed, soft turf felt under my feet. I also remember going to the driving range with my dad, and walking a few holes on the course with him. It was a great way for an eight-year-old boy to spend time with his father. That summer, Dad asked the club pro, Johnny Alberti, to cut down a couple of clubs to fit me. Every once in awhile he would let me pull my 6-iron out of his bag, and hit a ball up the fairway. I had to struggle to keep up with the big boys, but even at an early age I could already see that golf was a lot of fun. (My dad, who never threw anything away, kept that first 6-iron on his workbench until the day he died.)

At the time, I was also involved in Little League baseball. Because I was very small, my teammates had nicknamed me "Shorty." Even if I do say so myself, I was a damn fine second baseman. As the summers passed, I found myself going to the golf course more and more. Since both baseball and golf were typically summer sports, the conflict of the two forced me to make a decision. As much as I loved baseball, I knew that my heart was into golf. I had informed my dad at a very early age that I wanted to have a career in the game. When I was about 12, I stopped playing baseball. The thing I liked most about golf over baseball was that golf was an activity that I could do on my own. It is an endeavor in which you can enjoy the wonders of the great outdoors—various shades of green in the spring, the brilliant colors of summer, and the magnificence of autumn. With golf, your successes or failures are solely attributed to you. You don't have to rely on—or blame—anyone for either. And early in my life, I was an extremely shy young boy. So golf seemed perfect for me. And through the years, golf did help me grow out of this shyness.

In that first year of full-time commitment to golf, I was starting to see some progress in my playing ability. The first hole at The Brook was 300 yards long and there was a pretty deep bunker placed exactly 150 yards from the tee. When I first started playing, I couldn't even come close to that bunker with my tee shots. A year or so later, some of my drives were actually rolling into it. Eventually, near the end of my preteen years, one of my first golf dreams came true when I was finally able to carry that bunker with a tee shot. It was a very big deal for me because distance is everything when you're 12 years old. Once that major goal was accomplished, I moved on to bigger and better things.

The summer before I turned 13, I played golf nearly every day. My dad was able to get me a junior membership for $50 and I promised him that I would earn some money and pay him back. I was too young to caddie because you had to be 14, so I started picking up balls on the driving range, which was how I worked off my debt to my dad. Toward the end of the summer, I forged my working papers so I could be a caddie. By then I had the reputation of being a pretty decent golfer, so a lot of the good players wanted me to caddie for them. I would caddie in the morning and then play and practice until it got dark. I would then head for home by going down the big hill on the 18th hole, cut through some woods, and slip through a few backyards to reach my house. Caddying was a great education and it provided me with a wealth of experiences that would help shape me in future years.

The caddie master, Joe Frady, was one of the more colorful characters at The Brook. Joe had only one arm and I never worked up the courage to ask him how it happened. After completing your loop, the caddies were required to give Joe 25 cents. If you were smart, you gave him 50 cents. That way, you would get picked to caddie more often. Joe sold soda as an additional sideline and it was also a good idea to buy a lot of it. When you went to *play* at The Brook, if you needed a starting time you would slip Joe a couple of bucks and—magically—your time moved up on his starter's sheet. He had his own business operation going on there and it was a real eye-opener for a 12-year-old kid.

The caddie yard at The Brook, like caddie yards everywhere, was home to some memorable characters. My three favorites were J.T. Covington III, and two guys named Red. J.T. was a professional "looper" who caddied at The Brook in the summer and at The Breakers Hotel in Palm Beach, Florida, in the winter. He was actually a pretty good golfer, but he was better known around the yard for sometimes leaving his lunch, usually fried chicken, in the golf bag of the person he had caddied for. The odor-producing and offending evidence was often discovered a week or so later, much to the chagrin of the owner of the bag. The two Reds were distinguished by their physical characteristics and their attitude. One Red didn't have any teeth so he was called "No Teeth." The other guy had such a bad attitude that he was known as "Complainer." If you were asked where Red was, all you had to do to clarify the situation was to reply "No Teeth or Complainer?" Some of the other characters included Roach, Sonny Bop, Blue Boy, Mike the Weather Man, Tony Al, Lucky, and Gussie.

Every Monday, there would be eight guys on Joe Frady's starting sheet named Smith. Two foursomes, all named Smith. At first, I thought this was rather unusual. Although I never knew their real names, and I can assure you none of them were named Smith. Every week, two of the Smiths chose me to navigate them around The Brook. They were the absolute best loops. Almost all the golfers paid their caddies $5 per bag. Once in a great while, you might get $6. (A guy known as "The Rabbi" paid $4; you didn't want his bag.) For a Monday's work of caddying for the Smiths, I would receive $100. What a great feeling it was to have that crisp Ben Franklin in my pocket. All the other guys were dying to caddie for the Smiths and I was indeed fortunate to get more than my share of loops with them. I got to know all of the Smiths really well and I could club all of them accurately. I also had a lot of expertise in reading the tricky greens at Jumping Brook. And I promise you, my guys never had a bad lie in the rough. They were able to hit 3-woods out of four-inch grass, clover, and dandelions because I always got to the ball first. The Smith gang did not play for money. This was because, as one of them explained to me, "We choke when we play for dough." In lieu of playing for money, however, the loser always had to pick up the tab for dinner at restaurants such as Toots Shor's in New York City, where the bill might be close to a thousand dollars. If they didn't feel like making the trip into The Big Apple for dinner, they would play for golf balls instead. One day, one of the Smiths lost the bet and it cost him 1,100 dozen golf balls. That's right—1,100 dozen! The Smiths loved to "press" during their wagering (basically, double a particular bet), so it was not unusual for the losses to be heavy. I remember one time when they actually made a bet on whether or not a bird would fly out of a tree while they were on a tee! Thanks to the Smith gang, caddying was never boring.

On a number of occasions I caddied for a guy called "Big Jack." After looping for him a few times, someone at The Brook asked me if I ever watched "The Untouchables" on television. The program—about the FBI and the bad guys they were always putting in jail—was one of my favorites. Apparently, one of the characters on the show—a gangster who stood on a car's running boards, firing a Tommy gun—was patterned after Big Jack. After hearing this, I decided that it was in my best interest not to inquire about Big Jack's work history. Big Jack, shall we say, was slightly overweight. Between the wool shirt he always wore, the excess weight he carried, and the several scotches he had to drink before he teed off, he sweated more than anyone I had ever seen. It certainly did not help his game. One day I was carrying double for Big Jack and his very nearsighted playing partner, Little Ed. On the par-5 12th hole I was helping Jack look for his ball in the right rough. I had given Ed, who was in the left rough, his 3-wood so that he could work his way up the fairway. After helping Jack get out of the rough, I went over to see if I could help Ed. Before I could get to him, he addressed a mushroom and took a mighty swing. Because his eyesight was so poor, he thought he was hitting his golf ball. Broken pieces of mushroom went flying everywhere and Ed kept asking, "Where'd it go, where'd it go?" I had to be the bearer of bad news and say, "Sorry Ed, that was no Maxfli."

At one time or another I also caddied for Rocky Marciano, Vic Damone, and for the members of the singing group "The Four Seasons." There were also a lot of other intriguing people who showed up at The Brook, usually just to watch the action. One day a very attractive young woman followed the Smith gang around the course. Afterward, I thought she was introduced to me as "Mrs. Esner." Years later, I recognized her photograph in the newspaper and discovered that her real name was Judith Exner, an acquaintance of both President John F. Kennedy and the Chicago mobster Sam Giancana. Another time when I was caddying, I was alternating between walking and riding with a guy who had decided to take a cart. At the 14th hole, a shady-looking man showed up out of nowhere. He said to me, "Hey kid, take a walk." I started moving away and saw the guy getting into the cart with the guy I was working for. When he bent over to get in, I saw a gun under his coat and quickly picked up my pace. Fortunately, there was no report that day of any homicide at The Brook.

Once in awhile the Smith gang would have an "away match" and they would take their favorite caddie with them: me. A big Cadillac limo would pick me up at The Brook and we would be on our way. In addition to the $100 that I would always receive on these trips, I would also get several golf balls and all the pepper and egg sandwiches—one of my favorites—that I could eat. After I went away to college, my dad sent me several articles from the local paper, *The Asbury Park Press,* about the mobsters that the FBI had under surveillance at Jumping Brook. (I am certain that if those surveillance tapes still exist, I am right in the middle of a few of them.) The articles often contained transcripts of wiretapped phone calls and, since some of the Smith gang was involved, I read them with great interest. Several of those guys were eventually sent to prison and my services as a caddie were no longer needed.

In the summer of 1963, PGA Tour players Billy Casper and Julius Boros came to The Brook to play an exhibition match. The two other people who would complete the foursome were host pro Johnny Alberti and Dennis O'Keefe, an actor who played Ben Hogan's pal in the movie about Hogan's life called *Follow the Sun*. Casper and Boros were also scheduled to conduct a clinic before the match. It was my first chance to witness a clinic conducted by professional golfers and I was excited about it. Unfortunately, however, since I was picked to help shag balls for them, I had to watch the performance from quite a distance. When the clinic started, I was about 100 yards away with my fellow caddie Eddie Lee. Boros hit the first shot and cold-shanked it. Eddie and I were shocked. I said to him, "This guy won the U.S. Open?" Boros tried it again but hit another ugly shot. Not exactly an auspicious debut at The Brook for Mr. Boros.

After Casper and Boros finished their warm-up, Eddie and I made a beeline for their big, red and white Wilson Staff Bags. We flipped a coin to determine who would caddie for whom, and I won. I chose Billy Casper. Out on the course, I was amazed as I watched Casper hook his woods and fade his irons. I wanted to know what that was all about. What was most impressive, though, was that Casper made a lot of putts. He was phenomenal on the greens and I remember that it was a really great day. Another thing I learned was how nice these consummate professionals were and how well they were able to score. Casper missed a few shots but he was still right around par. Boros—after such a poor beginning on the range—shot 68. Boy, did those guys know how to get the ball in the hole. It was really a fun experience and it allowed me the opportunity to make some mental scoring notes that I could take advantage of in the future.

My best friend in those days was Tommy Jackson. He lived in the neighboring town of Wayside, but instead of caddying at The Brook he chose to caddy at Hollywood Golf Club. Tommy often told me how nice it was at Hollywood. At 16, and two years older than me, he was also the assistant caddie master at Hollywood. The job gave him playing privileges, and he frequently was able to work on his game or play during afternoons. The first time Tommy invited me to play Hollywood was on a Monday, or Caddies Day, and I simply couldn't believe how nice the course was. It was absolutely fantastic, and it's still my favorite of all the courses I've played. The original designer of Hollywood was Isaac Mackie, although many people mistakenly give the credit to Walter J. Travis. Actually, Travis was one of several notable architects—including A.W. Tillinghast, Dick Wilson, Geoffrey Cornish, and Rees Jones—who remodeled the course over the years.

When I was 15 I played in the State Caddie Championship, conducted annually by the New Jersey State Golf Association. The field consisted mostly of young golfers, but there were also a number of older men playing because they were full-time caddies. That year, as luck would have it, I hitched a ride with the caddie master from Hollywood Golf Club, Lou Accerra. On the way to the tournament, my friend Tommy sat in front next to Lou. Because I was fairly unknown to Lou, I was relegated to the backseat. I shot 74 that day and came in third. Lou, an excellent player, shot 75. Tommy was off his game and shot a 78. On the way home, I got to ride in the front seat next to Lou. At one point, he said to me, "Hey, kid, why don't you stop caddying at that cow pasture," referring to The Brook, "and come over to a real golf course and work for me? You'll be able to play the course on Mondays with the other caddies." That's how I got started at Hollywood. Man, I thought I'd died and gone to heaven!

Because there were so many caddies (about 50) at Hollywood they had developed quite an elaborate hierarchy. There was a caddie yard *and* a caddie shack, which had a lot of graffiti on the walls. While waiting for bags, we'd play cards, softball, and practice our chipping. Even though I was the new kid on the block, Lou gave me some good loops and got me out early. That was important because it gave me a chance to sneak on the course with Tommy in the afternoon to play a few holes. The club pro, Lou Barbaro, eventually caught us and said that the only way I could play the course in the afternoon was if I had a regular job at the club. I pleaded with him to hire me so that I could play golf on this wonderful course. He didn't really need any help but I think he could tell how important golf was to me, so he hired me on the spot to work with his two sons, Steven and Lou Jr., on the driving range. Many of the members lived in New York and traveled to New Jersey on the weekends. Since there wasn't much activity on the range during the week, Lou said we could hit balls as long as there weren't any members around. The Barbaro boys and I ended up hitting considerably more range balls than the members did.

On the range was a little log cabin that held all the range balls and other equipment that we used. It looked like it had been around since the days of Abraham Lincoln. We didn't have covered range pickers like they have today. All we had were scoopers that were basically baskets on the end of a golf club shaft. So, when we ran low on balls we would put on football helmets and go out and pick up balls, even while the members were hitting. After picking up the balls, the Barbaro brothers would put them in small baskets and take them back to the shack. I did it differently. Instead of a small basket, I used a huge yellow bucket. I also waited until the bucket was full before I carried it in, *and* I made sure that I was at the far end of the range when I was finished. Carrying that heavy bucketful of balls such a long distance really built up my arms, and I'm sure the added muscle helped my golf game.

In 1967 the U.S. Open was to be played at Baltusrol Country Club in Springfield, New Jersey. As a way of rewarding their caddies, several clubs in New Jersey were asked to send a certain number of their better caddies to work at the tournament (back then, players were not allowed to use their own caddie in the Open). Three caddies from Hollywood were chosen for this honor and I was one of them. To get ready for the Open, we had to attend caddie class at Baltusrol. One of the perks, though, was that we would be allowed to play the course on Mondays. In the spring of '67, on a few occasions, I used to cut school to take advantage of this perk.

The weekend before the Open all the caddies assembled at Baltusrol for the drawing to see which caddie got which bag. While we were waiting, the usual stories and lies were told. One guy told several stories about caddying for Arnold Palmer but no one believed him. That Saturday night I was reading a golf magazine and saw the caddie's photograph on one of the pages. His name was "Creamy" Caroline, and for years he had been Arnold's regular caddy. For this tournament, however, he was like the rest of us and his fate would be determined by the luck of the draw. Creamy was not happy when Don January drew his name — something of a personality clash, I believe. However, by the end of the week, after January finished third, Creamy had changed his tune. All week, Creamy regaled us with tale after tale. I especially liked his description of one of Arnold's five victories at the Bob Hope Dessert Classic and how proud he felt to be on the winner's bag. After hounding him for days for more stories, Creamy finally lost his patience with all of our questions and got ticked off. That was the end of story time.

The Tour pro who drew my name was Johnny Pott. The week before the Open, at the tournament in Memphis, he shot a 62 in the last round and finished second. I immediately began telling everyone who would listen that the team of Pott and Walters was really hot and we were going all the way. After meeting Johnny, I picked up his bag, a big red Spalding bag, and headed for the first tee for our opening practice round.

The first hole at Baltusrol is a long and difficult par 4 that is actually played as a par 5 by the members. Johnny hit a good drive and an excellent 4-iron, and then made the 20-foot putt. Birdie time. On the way to the second tee, he asked me about the next hole. I said, "Mr. Pott, it's an easy hole. Just hit a 2-iron off the tee to the top of the hill and all you will have left is a wedge or a 9-iron." I pulled the Spalding TopFlite 2-iron out of the bag and handed it to him. He hit a rifle shot right down the middle of the second fairway to the top of the hill. As I predicted, all he had left was a wedge, which he hit to within three feet of the pin. Another birdie. Visions of victory were dancing in my head. The third at Baltusrol is a dogleg left with woods along that side but it's not really the toughest hole in the world. Johnny snap-hooked his tee shot into the trees and said, "I drive the ball beautifully until I get to these U.S. Open courses." I knew right then we were in serious trouble. Unfortunately, instead of going all the way to victory, he birdied the last hole on Friday for a two-day total of 148, and missed the cut by one shot.

During our first practice round, Johnny mentioned that he was not happy with the way he was hitting his irons and that he wanted to work on his clubs. In those days, there wasn't an equipment van that traveled from tour stop to tour stop like there is today. Players who wanted to make changes to their clubs had to do it themselves. When we were finished with our practice, I carried the big golf bag into the club repair area, which was a dark little space in the cellar of the golf shop. Lo and behold, who do we run into in that cellar but the king himself: Arnold Palmer. He was wrapping new leather grips on his clubs. After the usual chitchat about each man's game, Johnny complained to Arnold that he was ballooning his long irons. Arnold suggested that Johnny put some lead tape toward the top of the irons. He then gave him some to see if it would help. A big thrill for me was when Johnny introduced me to Arnold as not only his caddie, but also as a young, "upcoming future champion." Arnold shook my hand and wished me luck with my golf game. That was something I will never forget. In my estimation, Arnold has done more to promote the game and set an example of good sportsmanship than anyone else.

Another thing that happened that made my Baltusrol experience very cool was the fact that Pott played the first two rounds of the tournament with Marty Fleckman. The young amateur shot a 67 in the first round and was leading the Open. In my scrapbook, I still have newspaper clippings that show me holding the flagstick for Marty.

Each day at the Open, even if my duties for Johnny were finished, I'd hang around Baltusrol. My graduation ceremony from Neptune High School was scheduled for that week, but I was too excited to think about it. I was more interested in watching Ben Hogan hit balls. One time when he was hitting balls, I was about

10 feet away, sitting directly behind him. I was wearing my caddie uniform which allowed me to sit inside the ropes. I just could not believe that anyone could hit the ball as well as he was hitting it that day. He was 55 years old at the time, but I doubt that I was even aware of it. I was so enthralled by his ball-striking ability, in fact, that I forgot that it was graduation day. I called my parents from the golf course and they told me that they would meet me at the auditorium with my cap and gown. When I got to the school, the graduates were in the process of receiving their diplomas in alphabetical order. It was a good thing that my last name started with W or I probably would have missed my graduation. Beneath my gown, I still had on my caddie clothing.

The next day at Baltusrol, Johnny and I finished our practice session early and it gave me a chance to watch Hogan again. I even got to see him play a few holes. Afterward, I decided to hang around the putting green for a while. To my surprise, I saw a player lying spread-eagle on the fringe of the green with his head resting on his bent arm. Since he was talking in Spanish to another player, I figured he had somehow miraculously qualified for the Open. There were four cups of beer alongside of him and he seemed to be having an absolute ball. However, I also remember thinking that the guy would probably shoot a million. But I was so intrigued that I decided to follow his progress during the tournament. I just needed to find out his name. It turned out to be Lee Trevino, and he ended up finishing fifth that year. In addition to seeing Trevino for the first time, I was also fortunate to be standing alongside the 18th fairway to witness Jack Nicklaus's famous 1-iron third shot on the 72nd hole that ensured his victory in that '67 Open. And the no-name Trevino would prove that it was no fluke by following it up in 1968 with his first U.S. Open triumph at Oak Hill in Rochester, New York.

That week was memorable for me in a number of ways, and it really got me fired up to play golf. Early on I had mentioned to Johnny Pott that I was an aspiring golfer and that I was working hard on my game. He surprised me by handing over six-dozen

Spalding Dot golf balls and I used them for the rest of the summer. Every time I hit one of those balls I felt as if I had a secret weapon. Later in the summer, I won the New Jersey Junior Championship, Caddie Championship, and Public Links Junior Championship. It was the first time that anyone had won those three events in the same year, and I'm proud to say that I'm still the only one to have ever done it. To my way of thinking, I had an advantage because I had a secret weapon: those Spalding Dots.

*   *   *

I played on the golf team in high school and enjoyed it very much. It was good experience and fun, too. We played our home matches at Jumping Brook, so that was a plus for me because I knew the course so well. Three of my teammates—Dicky Davis, Russ Walling, and Steve Young—were in my grade and were pretty good players. Our problem as a team was that we didn't have a reliable fifth man.

Par for the front nine at The Brook was 37, so naturally it was the more difficult nine to score on. Unfortunately, not that many people knew this. So, if any of us played the front nine in a match and shot 38 or 39, it didn't look too good in the sports section of the newspaper the next day. The back nine had a par of 35 and was considerably easier and we usually did not play it either in practice or in matches. Our coach, Walt Mischler, who usually phoned the scores in to the *Asbury Park Press,* had to leave early after completion of one of our matches and asked us to call in the results. This was too good an opportunity to let slip away. All of us were fans of the TV show *The Honeymooners,* so we decided to name our opponents after some of the characters on the program. I remember that I beat Ralph Cramden and Dicky beat Ed Norton, but I can't recall the other characters' names we used. During lunch at school the next day, we went to the main office to look at the sports section of the newspaper. Under the HS golf scores, there were the names just as we reported them. We were almost rolling on the floor with laughter. And since our coach didn't watch *The Honey-mooners,* he didn't have a clue about what was going on.

In my junior year in high school we qualified to play in the state tournament. Since none of us had played the course where it was to be held, we thought it would be helpful to get in a practice round. Believe it or not, we actually got permission from our parents to cut school and go check out the golf course. Steve and I met Dicky at his house (Russ didn't go for some reason) and we went to the tournament site from there. We had a great day and felt confident afterward that we would do well in the tournament. Driving home, we talked about how neat it was to have spent the day at a golf course rather than at school. Unbeknownst to us, our fun time was about to end. As we pulled up in front of Dicky's house, our high school principal, Mr. Coleman, who lived next door, turned in to his driveway. He caught his three high school golf stars red-handed. As punishment for skipping school—even though we had permission from our parents—Mr. Coleman barred us from going to the state tournament and sent the B team in our place. Our parents were outraged and the coach was beside himself, but Mr. Coleman would not change his mind. All these years later, I still believe that we would have won the state championship that year. I don't, however, have any hard feelings for what Mr. Coleman did. We broke a rule and there always has to be a consequence for anything you do wrong. To this day, part of me regrets our decision to go play that course . . . and part of me wishes we hadn't gotten caught. Who knows what would have happened?

Apparently, though, I didn't learn my lesson because that wasn't the only time I skipped school to play golf. The next time I did it—to play in a tournament—I did it without getting permission from my parents. The morning after, I wrote a note to my homeroom teacher that said I had been sick the day before. I then signed either my mother's or father's name and took the note with me to school. I thought I was being very clever. Unfortunately, after my homeroom teacher read the note, she immediately opened up the sports section of the local newspaper. She then read my note out loud to the entire class, followed by the names and scores from the tournament I had played in the day before. "You must have been sick yesterday," she said to me. "You shot a 78."

Caught red-handed again.

When I was 16, I played a kid named Billy Ziobro in the semi-finals of the New Jersey Junior Championship. He was the best player in the state at the time and eventually played several years on the PGA Tour. He only beat me 1-up that day but he put on an amazing display of short-game artistry. Billy had an old, brown-shafted Wilson R-90 wedge that had punch holes on the face. He used that club frequently and saved a lot of strokes with it. Thinking that a club like that might help my game, too, I decided to try and find one of those beauties. Hollywood Golf Club was my first stop. I asked Rocky Mara, who was in charge of the bag room, if I could look through all the bags to see if could find an R-90 and he agreed. There were about 200 bags in there and I went through every one of them. My thought was that if I got lucky enough and found one, I would ask the member whose bag it was in if I could borrow it. Well, I did get lucky and discovered one in the bag of a member named Robert L. Bier. This particular club was about 40 years old but it was in mint condition. The leather grip felt perfect and the clubface had lines on it instead of punch holes, which appealed to me even more. On the clubhead were the initials RLB. I asked Rocky if he knew anything about the owner. He told me that Mr. Bier had passed away but that a few of his family members used the clubs on occasion. My next question was whether Mr. Bier's family would mind if I adopted the wedge. Rocky thought it would probably be okay as long as I replaced the R-90 that I was taking with another similar club. Since I had an old Sandy Andy in my bag, I made the trade in a heartbeat and used that R-90 for the rest of my career. It was the best sand club I ever played with.

Whenever I think back on my teenage years I realize that I had many wonderful learning experiences. I also met a lot of interesting and influential people. One man who had a big influence on me during my youth was Lou Barbaro, the head pro at Hollywood

Golf Club. Not only was he a great player, he was a great *person.* His motto was: *It's nice to be important, but it's more important to be nice.* In the 1940s, Lou won a couple of tournaments on the PGA Tour. On his desk was an oversized sterling silver ashtray that he received for winning the Providence Rhode Island Open. It was a tour event in those days and all the big-name golfers played in it. Lou won the tournament by eight shots over Sam Snead. Ben Hogan finished *10* shots behind Snead. Lou also won two New Jersey Opens (1953 and 1959) when many of the top tour players also held jobs at prestigious golf clubs in the Jersey area. People told me that he was legendary for the way he hit his irons. They said that he was so accurate that if he played 36 holes in a day, many times during the afternoon round he would play out of his divots from the morning's round. In addition to the advice he gave me about golf, Lou taught me about other things, too. He had a tremendous, positive effect on my life and treated me like a son.

I have fond memories of growing up on the Jersey Shore. There were many good times on the golf courses, on the boardwalk, at the beach, and all the while eating the best thin-crusted pizza in the world at Mom's Kitchen in Neptune City. Nick and Dolly Alderelli, the owners of Mom's, are still some of my biggest fans and welcome me with open arms every time I get the opportunity to stop in. After my accident, thanks to my great memories of Hollywood Golf Club, I was able to get through some dark days in the hospital simply by replaying the course over and over again in my head. It was, and still is, a safe haven in my mind, a wonderful retreat from the real world.

– Chapter 4 –

College Life

THE UNIVERSITY OF NORTH TEXAS, formerly known as North Texas State University, is located in Denton, a short distance north of Dallas and Fort Worth. Before I became a student there, I had never been west of the Mississippi River. That fact made Texas seem very far from home. I had always heard that the best golfers were from Texas, so I wanted to go there to see if I could learn their secrets and improve my game. I also knew that I had to find a warmer climate than that of New Jersey so that I could play golf year-round.

I had won the New Jersey State Junior Championship and the State Public Links Junior, but college scholarships were hard to find. In those days, golfers were not heavily recruited. Instead, a network of alumni and former players was used by colleges and universities to identify possible prospects. Unfortunately, none of the schools in the Jersey area had approached me about a scholarship. Two friends of mine, however, Stan Mosel and Ray Ferguson, both club pros in New Jersey, were graduates of UNT. They were kind enough to put me in contact with the golf coach, Herb Ferrill.

I knew I was capable of playing for a major university and I knew UNT had a fine reputation. Its golf program was always ranked in the top 10 in the nation and I committed to go there without even making a visit—all it took to convince me were a couple of telephone conversations with coach Ferrill. He helped me to get a small scholarship to start with and we had an understanding that if I made the team, I would get more scholarship money. My scholarship *did* increase each year, and by the time I was a Junior I had pretty much earned a full ride.

The first time I played on the UNT golf course, I saw ground squirrels running all over the place. I had never seen anything like it. Believe me, there was a *big* difference between New Jersey squirrels and Texas squirrels. As you might guess, the squirrels in Texas were bigger and lived underground. It was kind of an eye-opener for me, and there was more to come. Fire ants, for example — creatures I didn't even know existed. Well, not only did they exist, they were so big that they had worn paths across the fairways. I saw a huge tarantula walking down the fairway once, too. He was a onesome and I guessed that nobody would play with him. As time went on and I saw more and more of these unusual sights, I began to realize that I had led a fairly sheltered life up to then. Clearly, I didn't know much about the world, or the creatures that lived in it.

The University Golf Course was just about the worst I had ever seen, but I was still happy to be there because I could play golf every day. It's hard to believe today, but it cost students 25 cents to play 18 holes and that was *overpriced.* There was one bunker on the whole course and because of it we called the place, "The Trap." The layout was perfectly flat, the ground was like concrete, and there were very few trees except for some small scrubby mesquite trees. Worse yet, the wind blew big-time. It was totally different from anything that I had ever experienced and it was a real shock to me. However, it turned out to be one of the best things that could have happened because it taught me how to play in the wind. I now had to adjust my game to playing conditions that were totally new. The toughest thing I had to learn was to hit the ball low. In New Jersey I had always hit the ball high. That wouldn't work in Texas. If you wanted to score low in Texas you had to keep the ball out of the wind. Punching the ball with my irons became one of the trademark shots that I eventually mastered to a certain degree. I was at the golf course every single day because I could practice and learn how to hit all these shots that I had never hit before. When I finally graduated in 1971, my mom asked me what I learned while I was in college. I remember my answer well. I said, "I learned how to hit a 2-iron off hard pan and also to keep my short irons down in the wind."

I met Guy Cullins in 1967 when we were both freshmen at UNT. Guy had been born in Pecos, Texas, but his dad was a PGA pro in Victoria, Texas, when we met. Guy's father eventually became a superintendent in Tyler, Texas. Not long after we met, Guy and I decided to room together and our friendship has lasted all these years. My other best friend at school was Ross Collins Jr., better known as "Rip." Rip was also the son of a PGA club professional, and he loved golf as much as Guy and I did.

Years later, Guy recalled those college days. "Dennis was there to play golf. He hardly ever missed a day. Our feeling was that we were in college basically to prepare ourselves to play on the PGA Tour. At first Dennis seemed a little lost and not real comfortable being in Texas. But he soon got over those feelings. He was a genuinely nice guy who loved golf and was living his dream. If there was something to be learned about golf, Dennis wanted to learn it. During the winter, on some of those cold, 38-degree days, a few of us would go out and play touch football. Not Dennis. He would be on the golf course hitting balls. I have no doubt in my mind that Dennis would have been a success on the PGA Tour."

It's true that I had to make a lot of adjustments living in Texas. Everyone on the golf team enjoyed making fun of my eating habits. I was a meat-and-potatoes kind of guy and I didn't like to mix together the food on my plate (I still don't). I didn't even like one food group to *touch* another one, which my teammates found hilarious. I also had never eaten chicken fried steak (a staple in Texas), much less even *heard* of it, and I had never eaten Mexican food either. To rectify this situation, the guys talked me into going to a local Mexican restaurant called "La Casita." Reluctantly, I tried the food. To my surprise, I liked it. The restaurant soon became one of my favorite spots to eat. We were eating there one time and, as usual, we were low on cash. This caused one of our teammates to suggest that we walk the check. "Walk the check," I'm embarrassed to say, means to simply leave without paying. We each slipped away, ostensibly to go to the bathroom, and then left through the back door. That night—I'm not kidding—the place burned to the ground. The next day, a wooden barrier was erected around the site and somebody put up a sign that read: Don't eat the food at La Casita, it's combustible. We often joked that we had run out of the restaurant so fast that the sparks from our shoes caused the building to catch on fire.

Besides my taste in food, another of my characteristics that my Texas teammates and friends felt was strange was my taste in music. When I was younger I had frequently caddied for two members of the singing group, The Four Seasons. Naturally, I had become a big fan of theirs. Well, the music by The Four Seasons (four guys from the East Coast) was not exactly what you'd call "Texas music" and I was forever being kidded about listening to it. A thief broke into my car while it was parked at the dorm one night and my tape deck and all of my tapes were stolen. Actually, all of my tapes except one: The Four Seasons tape. My buddy Guy told me, "Nobody in Texas wants that crap."

Fortunately, the thief also left behind a driver that I really cherished. Guy always said that it was the worst-looking driver in the world. He even named it "Doggy Brown," because he said the color of the clubhead looked like something that would come out of one end of a dog. Now, I can't deny that it was an ugly club. But I really loved it. Looking back at that situation should tell you something about my priorities at the time. It was okay that the tape deck was gone, but thank God the thief hadn't taken Doggy Brown or my Four Seasons tape.

The car that I was driving then was a 1963 Chevrolet Bel-Air. It was painted metallic blue, and we called it the "Time Bomb" because it made all these weird, ticking noises. We all thought it would blow up at any time. My sister, Barbara, had it first and she passed it on to me when I was a senior in high school. The reason I had the car with me was because I had gotten good grades during my first semester at North Texas (mainly because I had taken easy courses) and I had talked my parents into letting me take the car back to college after Christmas break. They agreed, but only on the condition that my dad would drive back to school with me and then return home by another means. So my dad and I left New Jersey and headed to Denton, stopping along the way to visit Barbara, who was attending East Tennessee State University. After leaving Barbara, we ran into a tremendous snowstorm near Knoxville and had to drive the rest of the way across Tennessee behind a snowplow that could only go 20 miles per hour. When we finally reached Denton, my dad was very happy that he had decided to drive back to Texas with me. I must confess that I was, too.

As good as I felt about my first semester grades, I should mention that math has never been my strong suit. As part of my course study at North Texas, I was required to take a trigonometry class and I did so in my second semester. The graduate assistant who taught the class was a certified golf nut and a part-time employee at the university golf course. After seeing how poor my math skills were but how good my golf swing was, he came up with a plan that would make both of us happy. As my part of the deal, I gave him golf lessons and golf balls. As his part of the deal, he told me, "Whatever you do, do not show up for my class."

It worked like a charm. I got a C in trig and he got a dramatically improved golf game. I'm sure it's safe to tell that story now because the statute of limitations must have run out several years ago.

*　　*　　*

One of the best things about going to school at UNT was the golf coach, Herb Ferrill and his wife, Mutt. When longtime UNT golf coach Fred Cobb died in the 1950s, Herb was appointed interim golf coach. For several years, he coached both football and golf. As time went on, though, the golf job became a permanent assignment. Coach Ferrill loved his golfers and he and Mutt always opened their house to us. Mutt was an excellent cook and we all knew where we could get the best meal in town. She was famous for her strawberry pie and she always made me one every time I visited her.

The Ferrills were an institution in Denton and the golf team was like their extended family. Every time we had matches or tournaments on the road, we traveled in two cars. On one of those trips, Miss Mutt decided that she would ride in the car that I was driving. When I was forced into a ditch by another vehicle, she scolded me mightily for not being more careful. It was the last time she rode in a student's car on a golf trip. Looking back, I'd have to say that Mutt was something of a surrogate mother to all of us on the golf team. There was also an element of innocence to those days in college, which I miss.

My first golf trip with the team was to Albuquerque, New Mexico, where we played in a tournament called The Tucker Intercollegiate. Two years later I tied for first in the Tucker with Bruce Lietzke, Andy North, and Ray Leach (Lietzke won the play-off). After that accomplishment I really felt that my game compared with those of the top college players in the country. One night during that first trip we went to dinner in downtown Albuquerque. While I was walking down the street a tumbleweed flew right over my head. I had never seen one. "Wow, what was that?" I asked. "I'm from New Jersey and we don't have low-flying projectiles like that."

When we traveled, Coach Ferrill knew exactly where to eat and sleep because he had made those trips year after year. We always stayed at the same cheap motels and ate at the same restaurants. He knew where every fried chicken place was in the Southwest and it seemed like every dinner we ate consisted of chicken. Having made so many of those trips, he also knew how to make the most of our $15-a-day food allowance. One year, at the NCAA tournament in Tucson, Arizona, he told us that he found a great place to stay. What he really liked, I'm sure, was that the rooms only cost $6 per day—a real bargain. The price was the reason the place was called "Motel 6," one of the first facilities in the chain that would eventually span the country. After we checked in, though, we learned that in order to watch television we had to put a quarter in a box on top of the set. This aspect of Coach Ferrill's "bargain" almost caused the team to revolt, but he solved the problem by giving each of us a roll of quarters.

The golf schedule at UNT usually called for us to play three or four tournaments in the fall and about eight in the spring. During my last two years on the team, I mostly played as the Number 2 or Number 3 man on the squad. Only occasionally did I play in the Number One position, but I do remember a match we had once with the Air Force Academy. It took place on our home course, "The Trap," and as usual the ground was like cement and the wind was blowing like crazy. Apparently, the guys from the service academy were not used to such extreme conditions because their high shots did not fare too well. After about six holes, one of the Air Force players said, "I can't wait until I am a senior and can go on a bombing raid. My first target will be this damn golf course."

The "Trap" had claimed another victim.

One of the funniest experiences from my college days occurred at a tournament held at Louisiana State University in Baton Rouge. Guy told me afterward that he saw Coach Ferrill at one point and was surprised to see Coach laughing. It was unusual because Coach was normally all business on the course. Guy asked him what was so funny and Coach said that he had gone over to the 13th hole to find out how I was doing. As a way of communicating with Coach on the course, we would use hand signals to let him know how much above or below par we were. Fingers up, over par. Fingers down, under par. When coach saw me at 13, he nodded to me to let him know how I was doing. I held up one finger, then a second, then the other two *and* my thumb. Thinking it meant that I was 5 over par, Coach started stomping around in frustration. When he looked at me again, I smiled and then turned my hand over so that all my fingers pointed down. He knew then that I was really 5 *under* par. Coach got the biggest kick out of this and couldn't wait to find Guy to tell him what I had done.

After I got out of college, I did my best to keep in touch with the Ferrills over the years. Following his retirement, Coach developed diabetes and eventually had to have a foot amputated. On one of my visits to see him later, we talked about how I might help him learn to play golf again. Mainly, I offered him encouragement and support. One time, I even challenged him to race me on his crutches to try to build up his spirits. I think that visit did him a lot of good. His spirits improved and he began to feel that it was possible to overcome almost any obstacle that life puts in front of you.

Eventually, Coach Ferrill passed away and it was one of the saddest days of my life. When I was inducted into the UNT Hall of Fame in 2000, the only thing that would have made the day more memorable would have been to have Coach Ferrill there. I still miss him a lot.

Years later, Mutt Ferrill remembered those college golf team days with affection. "My late husband and I loved those boys so much. It was different back then. The kids came here with hardly anything. No fancy clothes, and they weren't spoiled like so many of today's college golfers are. Dennis was the nicest boy and golf was his dream."

Playing college golf—traveling, spending time with teammates and friends—was the best time I ever had and I would not have traded it for anything. My golf game had greatly improved during those years, too. At that point in my life everything seemed to be falling into place.

– Chapter 5 –

"El Champo of
El Campo"

AT THE END of my junior year in college I decided to stay in Texas over the summer and play in as many golf tournaments as possible to gain more competitive experience. Texas was famous for its weekend golf tournaments. They were played all over the state, in large cities and small towns alike, and most of them included dinners and/or dances. Many of them were accompanied by a high-stakes Calcutta as well. This was a form of gambling through which bettors put up money to "own" a particular player in hopes of earning a big payout at the end of the tournament based upon that player's final standing. Golfers often referred to this collection of tournaments as the "Barbecue Circuit."

That summer of 1970, I entered the Texas State Amateur, which was held in Houston. There was a 36-hole cut in the 72-hole event and after shooting a two-round total of 149, I missed the chance to play on the weekend by one shot. I was both crushed and upset with myself for not making the final field, but it made me even more determined to play somewhere on the weekend. So I began looking for another tournament to enter. Someone at the Texas Amateur had told me that there were a number of small tournaments played on 9-hole courses and that there was a schedule of them in a publication called *Par Magazine*. So I picked up a copy, searched through the list, and found one in El Campo that seemed interesting. I telephoned the course to make sure they allowed college players in the event. Fortunately for me, they did.

To most people, El Campo, Texas, was nothing more than a tiny dot on a map, a town of about 10,000 people that was located near the Colorado River and the Gulf of Mexico. Founded in 1882, it was originally an old railroad camp that went by the names of Pearl Switch and Pearl of the Prairie before becoming El Campo ("The Camp"). Not surprisingly, the course where the event was to be played was called El Campo Country Club. Golfers, however, had another name for the layout: El Hard Pan. The reason was because the "watering system" at El Campo CC only covered the tees and greens and a single line down the center of the fairway. On either side of these green strips down the middle of the holes was a whitish/grayish soil that was common to the area. Local players knew that if they hit the ball there, it would roll forever.

I had no idea what the competition would be like since I didn't know a single player in the field. I assumed nobody knew me either, so I figured we were even. I played pretty steady the entire opening round and finished with what I thought was a pretty good score, a 3-under-par 69. Much to my surprise, however, I found myself standing in fourth place, three strokes behind the leader. Following the round, I went into a nearby trailer to look at the names of all the players on the Calcutta board. Several of them had been purchased for as much as $500. The "purse" for the event was the total amount of money spent to buy the players and it was all cold, hard cash. (I learned later that it was often in the area of $40,000 to $50,000.) Anyhow, when I finally found my name on the list, I also saw that I had been purchased for a whopping $40. Naturally, I wanted to know the name of the person who had such faith in me. "Oh," I was told, "it was the town drunk. When they got to your name, nobody had ever heard of you so somebody held up the guy's hand in order to continue on with the bidding."

Not what you'd call inspiring.

Over the first eight holes of the next day's second and final round, I struggled with my game and was standing at 2-over-par— six strokes behind the leader. Right about that point, a grizzled-looking older man pulled up beside our group in a golf cart. I had no idea who the guy was or what he wanted, but I knew it was going to get interesting because with him in the cart were two good-looking women and a couple of coolers full of beer. To my amazement, he introduced himself as the man who had bought me in the Calcutta the day before. After thanking him, I asked him if I could buy half of the action.

"Don't worry about a thing, son" he replied, slurring his words a bit. "I'll take good care of you."

With only 10 holes remaining to be played, I didn't think there was much hope that he would win back any of the money that he had wagered on me. If this worried my "backer," he didn't show it. People were constantly approaching him to make new wagers and doubling and redoubling existing bets. He happily obliged all comers and accepted every single wager. Even later, he never told me how much the bets totaled.

I really can't say for sure, but maybe that entire hilarious situation relaxed and motivated me at the same time. Regardless, I immediately began to play better. All I know is that I reeled off five consecutive birdies from the 10th to the 14th hole, and when I walked from the 17th green to the 18th tee, somebody informed me that I had a three-shot lead. Learning this, my goal then was to finish strong and make my new friend happy. Our group now had a gallery of 150 to 200 people following us. Many were in carts but most were just walking alongside. As I was walking up the hill to the elevated 18th tee, a middle-aged guy came right out of the gallery and put his arm around my shoulders. "Son," he said, pointing with his other hand to a spot some 200 to 300 yards well right of the tee box, "do you see those oil wells over there?" I told him I did.

"Well, I think we could raise a few thousand dollars to see if you could hit one."

I was glad that no one was close enough to hear what the man had said because the oil wells he was referring to were way out-of-bounds, and what he was suggesting was that I'd make more money by intentionally losing the tournament than I would by winning. Luckily for me, all my experiences from my New Jersey days came in handy at that moment. Nothing surprised me, and I did not get rattled at all by his comments.

"No can do," I promptly replied.

The 18th hole at El Campo was a medium-length par 5 of 539 yards. I absolutely killed my drive and split the middle of the fairway. In retrospect, I think the guy's offer on the tee spurred me on. I hit my second shot to just short of the green, chipped up and two-putted for an easy par. In winning the tournament with a total of 137 (69-68), my championship prize was a new set of aluminum-shafted First Flight irons. I knew that the last thing I was ever going to use was a set of aluminum-shafted irons, so within five minutes I had found someone in the gallery to purchase them for $100. Not long after, my Calcutta partner drove up in his cart.

"Let's go over to my car," he said. As he stepped out of the cart, I noticed that he was carrying a paper sack and that it appeared to be full of money. He'd clearly been guzzling a few of those beers, too, because he stumbled a bit as we walked to the car.

"Here you go," he said, emptying the sack of money on the front seat. "Split this up, will ya son? Make it one for you, one for me."

The entire pile was made up of $20 bills, and by the time I completed my role as banker, I had $3,100 in my stack. It might have been the most money I had seen at any one time in my life!

"Are you happy?" the man asked.

Boy-oh-boy, was I ever happy! I quickly nodded my head, took my pile of money, hopped in my car and immediately drove out of town. I'm serious when I say that the wad of bills was so thick, that it barely fit into my front pants pocket. My worry at the moment was that there might be some unhappy bettor laying low for me on the outskirts of town. Once down the road, I stopped at the first phone booth I saw and called my parents to tell them I had won a tournament.

"Did you win a nice trophy?" my mom asked.

"No," I said, "I won $3,100 in cash."

Both of them were flabbergasted. I usually talked to them every night when I was playing in a tournament, so they were not surprised by my phone call. They were, however, floored by the news. Being the wise old sage that he was, my dad advised me to go to the nearest bank and get the money changed into travelers' checks. It was a Sunday, though, and I would have to guard the money until the next morning.

Bill Wiley, one of my college teammates, lived in nearby Victoria, Texas. Before the tournament at El Campo, I had made plans to drive to his place when it was over and spend the night. When I got there, Bill greeted me warmly then asked, "Well, how did you do?"

"I did OK," I said, as nonchalantly as I could, and then tossed the wad of bills to him. He was speechless.

First thing the next day, Bill took me down to the local bank so I could change the cash into travelers' checks to appease my dad. I walked up to the teller and told her that I wanted $3,000 in traveler's checks. When she asked me how I would pay for them, I pulled the wad of bills out of my pocket and placed it on the counter. To say the least, she was taken aback. Once she regained her composure, she had me complete all the paperwork and off I went with a new booklet of travelers' checks. I used that money all summer long, traveling to amateur events around the country.

Even today, there are people in El Campo who remember the wild and wooly tournament that took place in 1970. Tim Supak, a lifelong resident who now oversees the entire golf operation at the club, is convinced that the person who purchased me in the Calcutta was a rice farmer by the name of John Clipson. "Vernon Roy was the tournament director at the time and he told me it was Clipson," Supak says. "He (Clipson) and a couple of other 'characters' spent thousands of dollars on players in the Calcutta. The man who came out of the gallery to try and entice Dennis into hitting it into the oil field had to be a guy named Johnny Zapalac. He's the only one that had enough nerve to do that. All these guys knew each other very well and were good friends. There was nothing they enjoyed more than taking one another's money.

"Vernon Roy's son, Pat, caddied for Dennis in that tournament. When it was over and Dennis was getting ready to leave, he handed Pat $50. It was more money than he had ever seen.

"People who are still around remember Dennis," says Supak. "He was about as good a player as they had ever seen play here. It was years later when we heard about the accident. We were all sorry to hear what happened because it was evident to everyone around here that Dennis was good enough that he would have made it out on Tour."

That trip to El Campo was the one and only time I have been in the town. Ironically, 20 or so years later I met someone from the town who remembered seeing me win the tournament. I asked him if they still held the event.

"Yes," the man said, "It's still held every year. But since you won it, they don't allow college players to participate any more."

Which, in myth, if not in fact, seems to make me the enduring El Champo of El Campo.

* * *

Soon after I graduated from college in 1971, I decided one day that I wanted to spend some time in Florida. So in January of 1972 I drove to West Palm Beach and met up with a Canadian friend of mine, Greg Pidlaski. Greg, like me, was a golf nut. We soon found a garage apartment on New York Avenue to rent, not too far from the West Palm Beach Country Club, where we played golf during the daytime. To help pay expenses, we got jobs parking cars at Manero's Steak House. Tony Manero had won the 1936 U.S. Open at Baltusrol Country Club in New Jersey, so we thought it was very cool that we were working at a restaurant bearing his name. A fringe benefit of working there was that we got to park the cars of some famous golfers, such as Jack Nicklaus, Sam Snead, Toney Penna, and Toney's buddy, Perry Como. A benefit of living in the area was that we could always get a good game at West Palm Beach Country Club.

That first visit to Florida was just about a perfect situation. We played golf all day and parked cars at night. Our living arrangements, to say the least, gave us a few laughs. One of the funniest things that I remember about that time was the heater in the apartment. Every time we turned on the heater, flames shot out of it. We nicknamed it the "Flame Thrower." Fortunately, it never got that cold in West Palm Beach so we didn't have to risk our lives too often. Every month we paid our rent in one-dollar bills, our tip money from the restaurant. The landlady, Dolly, loved us and said we were her favorite tenants.

After spending the whole winter in Florida, I returned to New Jersey and went to work for Lou Barbaro, the professional at Hollywood Golf Club and my longtime mentor. It was great because Hollywood was where I had caddied and worked on the range when I was going to Neptune High School. That summer of 1972 was also when I lost the New Jersey Open in a play-off. I learned a lot as an assistant pro from Lou, but my long-term goal never changed: I wanted to gain as much tournament experience as possible and make it on the PGA Tour.

In the fall of that year, I played in my first PGA Tour Qualifying school. I didn't have any problem getting through the initial stages, but the later rounds were much tougher than I expected and I didn't make it through. That lack of success told me that I needed more tournament experience as a pro, so I started playing in any event I could find. It wasn't so easy back then because there weren't many choices. I played on a few of the early minitours in Florida, and competed in some small tournaments in Canada and the United States. One of them was the Egg City Open in Pittsfield, Maine, where I finished second. My prize was a choice of either 500-dozen eggs or $500 in cash. I took the cash. I figured since

Pittsfield had the reputation for having the world's largest frying pan, its residents needed the eggs more than I did.

During that tournament in Maine I stayed with my friend Roger Ross and his family. One day Roger introduced me to a friend of his. It was Sandy Koufax, the retired Hall of Fame baseball pitcher for the Los Angeles Dodgers. Without question, Sandy was one of the finest left-handers of all time. After I met him, we played a little golf and I found out that he was pretty good at that, too. The chance to play golf with one of my heroes and then have a beer with him after the round was hard to beat.

During one of our rounds, Sandy noticed the old RLB sand wedge in my bag and pulled it out. After swinging it a few times, he said, "If you ever see one of these for a lefty, let me know."

There was something special about that wedge.

*   *   *

Because there were so few opportunities for me to compete in the United States, I decided in the fall of 1973 to go to South Africa and play on the tour there. I was willing to do anything to improve my game, and I knew that the additional experience and confidence building that I could gain there would be invaluable.

Living and playing in South Africa turned out to be fantastic. Among the many great golfers I was able to play with were Bobby Locke, Gary Player, Harold Henning, Bobby Cole, Peter Oosterhuis, and Simon Hobday. I also met a teenage phenom from Rhodesia named Nick Price, who would go on to win a British Open Championship and two PGA Championships.

I was lucky enough to go 18 holes with Gary Player eight or nine times, either in practice or competition. The first time I was paired with him in a tournament was the most memorable. Simon Hobday, who would one day win the U.S. Senior Open, was also in our group. Hobday, a "character" to say the least, decided that it should be our goal (his and mine) to beat Gary. As Simon put it to me, "Let's beat this little S.O.B." Gary, who had already won all four of golf's major championships, was a sporting deity in South Africa, his home country. On the second hole of the first round, I hit my ball into a greenside bunker. Player's ball was in the same bunker, only a few feet away from mine. Regarded as one of the finest sand players of all time, Gary hit his bunker shot within three feet of the hole. He then watched as I almost holed my shot, the ball stopping a foot from the cup. He picked up my old RLB wedge to check it out and told me that it was "a beauty." We continued the round and by the end of the day I had beaten Player by one stroke, 72 to 73. Fortunately, I saved the scorecard. Several years later, I saw Gary again and asked him to sign it. Next to his signature he wrote, "Fair and square."

There was a shop in downtown Johannesburg called the Golf Club Exchange where I spent a great deal of time. It was located in the basement of a store, two floors below the street level, and was so dark and dusty that at first I almost decided not to venture down there. That would have been a huge mistake. Among the filth and cobwebs was a treasure trove of goodies. Some of the most beautiful and rare MacGregor drivers I had ever seen magically appeared before my eyes. I couldn't believe what I was seeing. Most of the woods were in mint condition, and there were hundreds to choose from. I finally culled them all down to the 50 or so that I wanted to buy. Before I left South Africa to head for home, I removed the shafts and stuffed the heads in my suitcases and golf bag. On an earlier visit to the store, I made another special discovery. I found a left-handed model of my RLB sand wedge that Sandy Koufax so admired. I gave it to him when I returned to America and he was pretty excited about it.

Another person I met in South Africa (and to this day we're still close friends) was Ed Holding. Today, Ed is one of the most highly respected head professionals in South Africa. Back then, though, he was a young assistant professional at the Wanderers Club in Johannesburg. The Club was the site of the 1973 South African PGA Championship, and that tournament was the first event that I played in on the Sunshine Circuit. When I arrived there, Ed was the first person I met. So immediate was our friendship that Ed invited me to stay at his parents' home while the two of us followed the South African golf circuit. I loved staying at Ed's. His parents treated me like I was part of the family, and he had a very cute dog named Nero. Since I had always been a dog lover, Nero—a Kerry Blue terrier—and I became instant buddies. One of the things I enjoyed most about Nero was a trick that Ed had taught him. He would point his finger at the dog and say "Die for your country." Nero would then roll over onto his back and put all four paws in the air. I never got tired of watching Nero do that trick (although I'm sure *he* was pretty tired of doing it by the time I left South Africa).

Ed and I became like brothers. His nickname was "Grave Digger" because he made such huge divots whenever he was practicing. When he and I talk about our days in South Africa together, Ed has vivid memories and mental pictures of me standing on the range pounding golf balls and walking around the course. We were dedicated athletes making sure that we jogged or went to the gym every day. We also—as the old saying goes—"hit golf balls until our hands bled." Golf was a religion to us in those days and we gave it our all. We never went to bars or nightclubs but we did have a vice: we made a daily visit to the local ice cream store. Obviously, we lived, ate, drank, and slept golf.

We couldn't wait to get to the golf course in the morning, and we hated to leave when the sun was going down. The conditions were perfect in South Africa the year-round, with virtually no wind or humidity to contend with except in the coastal areas where the wind was unbelievably strong. South Africans are fond of saying that in coastal towns like Port Elizabeth, it is so windy that the birds walk. If you were a keen player, the opportunity was there to become a great golfer. Perhaps that's why South Africa has produced so many. In the 1970s it was the training ground for young players from America and Europe. It was inexpensive to live there, it was competitive, and it was a great tour to play on. Also nice was the camaraderie among all of the golfers. The atmosphere was very laid-back, and nowhere near the dog-eat-dog kind of situation that might have been common on other tours. I was grateful for that.

I played about a dozen tournaments in South Africa and the experience of competing with so many outstanding golfers really helped my game. I felt very good about it, and about the fact that I had adjusted so well to living and playing in another country. Although, perhaps *too* well. When I returned to the United States eight months later, the first time I drove my car I headed down the wrong side of the road. My brain was still in South Africa.

Overall, I was very pleased with my game and my experiences during 1973. It made me look forward to the following year with confidence—and another chance at my dream of playing on the PGA Tour.

Little did I know that a short time later that dream would be shattered forever.

– Chapter 6 –

"You'll Never Play Golf Again"

AFTER FIVE WEEKS AT Morristown Memorial Hospital, I still could not feel or move my legs. I was really discouraged by my situation. One day I spent hours trying to move one of my big toes. I figured that if I could move my toe, maybe something else would start to work as well. I only had a sheet covering me, but I tried so hard for so long that I got really sweaty. Suddenly, the sheet moved. I yelled out, "Holy shit, I moved my toe!" A doctor rushed in and asked me to do it again. I couldn't, of course, so he told me that I must have had a spasm. I asked him what that was and he said it was an "involuntary muscle movement." He also told me to expect more of them, and not to let my hopes get too high.

In a matter of minutes, I went from the elation of thinking that movement was coming back, to a deeper, darker, bubble-bursting depression.

Not long after I'd been admitted, I was moved into a private room near a nurse's station. Because of my condition, I was put in a mechanical bed called a "striker frame bed." Its purpose was to allow certain patients to be frequently flipped from back to front by rotating the inner part of the bed. This was done every three hours to prevent the patient from getting bedsores. I grew to hate it when the nurse would come in and begin to prepare me for the flip. The procedure went as follows: If I was lying on my back, the nurse would insert a narrow board into a slot in the bed frame that was very close to the front of my body. The bed's motor was then started and the rotation would begin. The motor made a loud grinding noise that reminded me of fingernails being scraped across a chalkboard. I learned to hate that sound. Once I was flipped over, I would lie on the narrow board that came to just under my chin, facing down and staring at the floor. In a couple of hours, the procedure would be reversed and I would again be lying on my back on the mattress of the bed. The whole time I was stuck in that bed, I never got a full night's sleep.

Finally, after being confined to bed for six weeks, I was able to get into a wheelchair. During that time, it had been hard for me to get a good look at my bed. In my mind I had pictured it as being sort of a four-poster bed with a chrome canopy. Now, from the wheelchair, I could see how wrong I'd been. My "home" for the previous six weeks looked like some kind of a monstrosity with two big Ferris-wheel-like contraptions on either side of the bed. As I gazed at it for the first time, it was one of the most frightening-looking things I'd ever seen. And I was sure that everyone who had come to visit me over those first few weeks was deeply affected by the sight.

I constantly asked any hospital staff member who came into my room if I would get better and how long would it take. I got the same answer almost every time: "It usually takes six to eight weeks for the swelling on your spinal cord to go down. If and when that happens, recovery is a possibility."

As I think about it now, I believe the doctors were sure the paralysis was permanent, but they never told me that. My doctors would come in every day and jab me with straight pins and ask me if I could feel anything. Because my answer was always "No," I began to lose hope and became more scared and depressed. For me, it was the worst of times.

The strange thing about this injury was that I was never in much pain. Even today, the only pain I have is the unrelenting pins-and-needles feeling that runs up and down my legs. It is particularly painful on the bottoms of my feet. After 27 years, I have accepted this pain and long ago started to ignore it and have somehow learned to live with it. It's not easy, however, and I would certainly trade places if I had a choice.

At some point during my stay at Morristown Memorial I was fitted with a brace that looked like a chest protector that a base-ball catcher would wear, except that it was open in the middle and it had metal bars on either side. The brace extended from my chin down to just below my belly button. I distinctly remember how uncomfortable it was because it was covering one of the few parts of my body that I could actually feel. I was in that brace 24 hours a day, seven days a week. I was told the device was necessary and an important part of my surgical recovery. With some injuries similar to mine, a steel rod is implanted in the back to stabilize the spinal cord. In my case, it wasn't an option. All they could do was clean up the area around the affected vertebrae at the T-12 level, and put me in the brace. The purpose of the brace was to provide me with some stability and to prevent any twisting or turning.

The whole time I was at Morristown Memorial my biggest hope was that my nightmare would go away. After six weeks my fears were still strong, but my hopes went up slightly when they told me that I was being transferred to the Kessler Institute for Rehabilitation in West Orange, New Jersey. Kessler Institute, the doctors said, was one of the most renowned rehab hospitals in the world. Everyone I talked to said that wonderful things were being done there. I assumed that "wonderful things" meant that they were going to fix me up and get me back on my feet again. In my mind, I figured that a hospital was where someone recovered from surgery, and a rehab facility was where someone learned to walk again. Unfortunately, it took me a long, long time to realize that there isn't a rehabilitation facility in the world that can help some-one if they have no control of their muscles. At the time I was transferred to Kessler, I didn't comprehend this. It was much later before I understood that, in my case, rehabilitation really meant that they were going to teach me how to live as a paraplegic and give me the tools to function on a daily basis. Their plans for me included learning how to operate a wheelchair, drive a car, and contend with the challenges of daily living. Perhaps it was denial, but even while I was learning these tasks, I still did not realize that I had been given a life sentence without parole. It was a time of total bewilderment.

On my last day at Morristown Memorial before my transfer to Kessler, the nurses decided to give me my first shower in six weeks. I was placed on a stretcher and rolled into a large stall-like shower. I felt better immediately because I didn't have that damned brace on. The *best* feeling, however, was when the warm water splashed down on my head and rolled along my neck and shoulders. That good feeling continued as the water ran down my chest and stomach, but it stopped suddenly when it reached my lower extremities. I still couldn't believe that I couldn't feel my legs.

*   *   *

When I arrived at Kessler by ambulance, I entered the facility not quite knowing what to expect. Both literally and figuratively, I entered the world of rehab on the ground floor. That may sound silly, but because I had never been in a wheelchair before, I needed a few lessons—especially since I couldn't feel or move my legs. My first and most important bit of advice was given to me by one of my fellow patients.

"You have to watch out that your foot doesn't fall off the foot rest," he said. "Because if it does, you'll run over it and then you'll be more messed up than you already are."

It was good advice and I have followed that recommendation every day since, constantly checking to make sure my feet are okay whenever I am in my wheelchair. One of the first tasks that I had to undertake was to learn how to transfer my body from my bed to the wheelchair and vice versa. This process involved putting a small 2-foot long board between the bed and the wheelchair. This board is sometimes called a "slide board" because when you use it, you sit on it and then slide across it to get into either the bed or the wheelchair. When I first saw it, I thought it might be a surfboard for a squirrel. This board can also be used to transfer from a wheelchair to a car. Early on, I learned that having strong arms would be a tremendous asset. Lifting one's dead legs up and down a hundred times or so a day can be very tiring. I was fortunate that my arms were already pretty strong, which helped a lot, but I decided that I needed to build them up even more.

Getting dressed every day was something that I had never thought much about before my accident. I'd simply put on my underwear, socks, shirt, pants, and shoes and be on my way. The first time I tried this simple task by myself in rehab, it took me about 30 minutes. Trying to get dressed while lying down involves picking up one leg at a time and shoving it into your pant leg. Once you get your legs in the pants, pulling the pants up requires a series of twists and turns and pulls and pushes until somehow your pants are on and near your waist. In essence, if you think about it, my body is cut in half. The top half feels perfectly normal, but I have no feeling at all in the bottom half.

Paralysis also screws up all of your internal body functions. It's not just a matter of being unable to walk; there's much more to it than that. Losing control of your bowels and bladder also means losing your dignity, and that has a *tremendous* negative effect on your self-image. Many times early on I thought to myself, *I could handle this if I didn't have to deal with these two problems.* When I was at Morristown Memorial, a catheter was put inside me to control my bladder function. Since I had no feeling down there, the device didn't cause me any physical discomfort. However, just looking down at the hookup caused me immense mental anguish. After I got to Kessler, though, the decision was made to remove the internal catheter and replace it with an external one. Two attempts to accomplish this were made but both failed. On the third try, a different brand called the Texas Catheter was used and the doctors were successful. Since I considered Texas my second home,

I was elated when my bladder cooperated and the catheter worked. I have continued to use the Texas Catheter for the last 27 years.

This catheter business was hardly anything to laugh about at the time, but it did give me a humorous moment one day. I was cruising down a hallway in my wheelchair when I noticed a closet door was open. I looked inside and all I could see were cases of Trojan condoms. *Wow!* I thought. *What an awesome place.* It turned out that condoms were sometimes used to make a sort of homemade external catheter. I thought that was pretty funny.

Problems with my bowels was another messy situation that I had to learn how to deal with. At the Institute, I was given a suppository three times a week. If you've never had one, I can only tell you it is a miserable experience to go through—especially on a regular basis. Sometimes it worked for me, sometimes it didn't. I awoke on more than one occasion only to realize that I had had a bowel movement. I didn't know it because I couldn't feel it. Since those early days at Kessler, I've had to become more attuned to my body and what is happening inside of it. Most of the time I get a sensation that lets me know when I have to have a bowel movement. Unfortunately, I can't stop it or control it. The result is usually a mad rush to make it to the bathroom in time. I usually make it, but not always. Make it or not, it's still a depressing situation that I have to deal with day after day.

After a couple of months at Kessler without any improvement, I pretty much concluded that my situation was going to be permanent. However, I still needed to talk to someone and get a final medical opinion. I asked my attending doctor point-blank if I would ever walk. He thought for a moment and then let the guillotine blade drop. "No, you'll never walk again," he said. His reply penetrated me like a knife and I burst into an uncontrollable fit of tears. Up until that point, I had guarded my emotions very carefully. In the darkest of times, I had always conjured up an image of me walking down an emerald green fairway, hitting the ball long and straight. It helped calm my fears. Unfortunately, my doctor wasn't finished. "Not only will you never walk again," this medical moron said, adding insult to injury, "you'll never play golf again."

His comment made me furious, perhaps for the first time since that awful July day. I stopped crying immediately and my emotions turned to outright rage. "You sorry son of a bitch!" I shouted. "I'm coming back to this damn place some day and I'm going to hit golf balls right off your front lawn!" Shortly after that encounter, Red Hoffman, the legendary golf writer for the *Newark Star-Ledger,* called to chat and get an update on my condition so that he could continue to let the readers know how I was doing. I told him about my conversation with the doctor and about my determination to prove that bastard wrong.

One day during one of my worst periods at Kessler, I was so depressed about my lack of progress that I could hardly roll my wheelchair back to my room. Before I could transfer myself into bed, though, I saw a letter sitting on the night table. I picked it up and saw that the return address was from Ben Hogan, my absolute hero. Mr. Hogan had been in a near-fatal car accident many years earlier and he often sent letters of encouragement to others in similar situations. Not many people knew of these acts of kindness because he was such a private person and because he didn't want the media to know. Believe me, his letter was far better medicine for me than any pill or potion. The words of encouragement really lifted my spirits. If nature had allowed it, I think I could have flown.

Additional letters and cards that I received during my stays at both Morristown Memorial and Kessler kept me going emotionally. I got a handwritten letter from Jack Nicklaus and a giant get-well card from the PGA Tour that had been signed by all the players. Many of the Tour players also sent individual cards and notes. The award for the most entertaining visit by a PGA Tour player went to Joe Inman, who never stopped talking and kept the hospital staff and me in stitches the whole time he was at Morristown Memorial. My friend Ralph Terry also got some Major League baseball greats such as Mickey Mantle, Whitey Ford, Joe DiMaggio, and Yogi Berra to send cards and sign memorabilia.

All of it helped keep me upbeat.

I was working out as much as I could, spending about two hours a day building up my arms by lifting weights and stretching. I was not satisfied with just strengthening my upper body; I wanted more. One day during group therapy, my therapist, Joe Powell, asked if anyone would like to try to stand up. I immediately raised my hand (the only one in the group to do so). Not only would Joe's offer give me more time in the gym, it would give me my first opportunity to be upright in months. Joe was elated to have a volunteer. It was the beginning of the next phase of my recovery.

In order for me to stand, Joe put rubber splints on my legs and then wrapped an ace bandage around my lower body from my waist to my ankles. This secured the splints and helped keep them rigid. With my wheelchair locked in place at the end of a set of parallel bars and my legs sticking straight out in front of me, I grabbed the bars above my head and hoisted myself up straight. It was really weird the first time I did it. I felt as if I were 10 feet tall because it was the first time I had stood in almost three months. However, since I could not feel my legs, I also felt as if I were suspended in midair.

Using my hands and arms, I hauled my way up and down the length of the parallel bars for a couple of weeks and became quite adept at it. Joe then decided that it was time for me to try the same routine but with crutches instead of the bars. "Let's give these a try," he said, handing me a pair of heavy wooden crutches. It turned out to be very difficult, and I was soon complaining because the heavy crutches were killing my arms. After about a week of listening to my moaning and groaning, Joe switched me to a pair of Canadian crutches—you know, the kind that were much lighter and that could also be attached to my forearms.

Day after day, Joe and I went up and down the halls. I got pretty good at using the crutches and my self-esteem improved because I felt great standing up and looking people straight in the eye. Being upright more was also good for my internal organs because the body will function much better if it is not in a sitting position all of the time. Eventually Joe decided it was time to move outside. This change of scenery presented me with a whole new series of navigational challenges. Inside the Institute the hallways were smooth and level. Once outside, I quickly learned that there were very few level places to be found. On my first attempt at "walking" outside, I hit a little bump and fell flat on my face. That led to a new challenge centered on the correct way to fall and how to get up once I hit the ground. Without the use of your legs, getting up by yourself is almost impossible and very frustrating. But with a lot of practice and some expert advice from Joe, I was able to master this task.

I continued to learn all about the intricacies of walking with braces and crutches. Getting around like that was extremely difficult and it took all of the strength I had. Although it was technically called "walking," in reality what I was really doing was getting around through the use of my arms and hands. My main motivation for learning how to do it was to figure out a way to be able to putt. Once I got good at standing, I began balancing myself on one crutch so that I could putt one-handed. It was another in a long line of challenges. But just being able to stand up was definitely good for me both physically *and* mentally.

During my last month at Kessler I was fitted with a pair of leg braces that were long, heavy, and made out of metal. Worse yet, they were attached to *the* ugliest pair of orthopedic shoes that anybody could ever imagine. The moment I saw them, my goal was to get rid of them as soon as I could and replace them with a pair of Foot-Joys.

As day after day went by without any sign of recovery, my hope for a miracle became dimmer and dimmer. My dream of recovery never came true. Twenty-five years later I did meet a man with a similar type of injury, but he had better results. Mike Franz, an executive with Sprint, the communications company, was an avid golfer. After an accident that left him paralyzed, he, too, dreamed that he was going to recover and get back on the golf course. One day, miraculously, he was able to move one of his big toes. More feeling and movement gradually returned to the rest of his legs.

He was soon standing up using braces and he got stronger each day. Eventually, he no longer needed braces and crutches and got around with a walker and then just a cane. In total, his recovery took about six months. Meeting him today, you would never even know that he had once been unable to walk. *His* dream came true.

In spite of some of the advances I made while I was at Kessler, my time there was as bad a period in my life as I have ever experienced. The stark realization that I would never walk again was with me daily and I hated almost everything about my life. Rarely did I find anything to smile or laugh about. I was so miserable I even developed an alter ego to help me cope with the nightmare that I was living. I called him "Mr. Crippee," and I wished that all the bad things that had happened to me—and were happening—would happen to him instead. I really despised "Mr. Crippee." I'm not sure if this helped, but at least it was an attempt to try and move on with my life as best as I could.

– Chapter 7 –

Repairman

AT THE KESSLER INSTITUTE, learning to repair watches was considered one of the premier job possibilities for someone in my condition. The thinking—and there was nothing wrong with it; the staff was only trying to help people like me find a way to make a living—was that even though I could not use my legs, my arms and hands were just fine. Therefore, I could still do something useful.

Well, I can tell you that I *hated* the whole concept of repairing watches. *Hated* it. And every day I resisted efforts by the staff to get me interested in this type of job training. I was also not interested in putting round pegs in square holes, making ashtrays, or going for psychiatric counseling. Looking back, I'm sure I felt that it was up to me to find solutions to my life's problems. At the time, my sole interest was in physical therapy. And physical therapy to me meant working out all day long, stopping only long enough to eat. The physical therapists, however, thought otherwise. After only an hour or two, they would tell me to leave the gym. This was very frustrating. The most frustrating thing of all was that I never got the chance to rehabilitate my legs. I always dreamed that my legs would return to normal one muscle group at a time, and that I would gradually regain their total function. I visualized my legs becoming so strong, in fact, that I even thought about running marathons some day. But it never happened. And my legs remained two lifeless appendages at the south end of my body. For someone who had always been so active and lively, just looking at or touching my dead, useless legs totally repulsed me.

Today, I frequently laugh about my potential watch-repair career with my good friend Wayne Warms. Back then, though, the thought of fixing watches made me very angry. So Wayne, wisely, used it to motivate me. What happened was that one of the organizations or companies that hired physically challenged people to do watch repair somehow got my name and sent me a letter, encouraging me to consider that as a career. To say that the whole thing did not sit well with me is an understatement.

"Dennis was furious," Wayne says today. "He ripped up the letter and told me that he was *not* going to sit in a chair all day fixing watches."

Some time later, during one of my many periods of extreme depression, I received a package in the mail from Wayne. I opened it and lo and behold, there was a watch inside. An accompanying note read: Fix me. I knew immediately that Wayne was trying to motivate me by making me angry all over again. And it worked.

"That got him going," Wayne recalls. "It was the biggest insult possible at the time. To Dennis, that watch was a symbol of giving up."

Looking back on it, I can see that Wayne's not-so-subtle hint pushed me to continue the process of bettering myself—both mentally and physically—just as he had hoped. And hitting golf balls was the first step.

After I was in rehab for a while, I was allowed to spend the weekends at my parents' condo in Freehold, New Jersey. There was a clubhouse in their development, and inside one of the rooms there was a net set up so that residents could hit golf balls during the winter. One weekend, my dad and I were watching a golf tournament on television and I started crying. I told him that I really missed hitting golf balls.

My dad said, "Damn it, if you can't stand up and hit a golf ball, let's go see if you can hit one from that freakin' wheelchair." That's when it all started.

At first, sitting in my chair, I couldn't swing a club without hitting my legs. We solved that problem by getting me a huge pillow to sit on. When I did, I was able to clear my legs and not hit them when I swung the club. We also attached a waist strap for balance and also so I would not fall out of the wheelchair, and then anchored the chair with ropes tied to a metal ring on the floor. My dad did all of the work in setting this up and he was always experimenting with one thing or another to make it easier for me. After some trial and error and a few practice sessions, I got to where I could hit the ball into the net fairly solid on a regular basis. Believe me, the loud WHACK I heard when I hit the ball was music to my ears. It was a sound that I thought I would never make again. Yet as great as all this was, I still wasn't satisfied. Since we were indoors, I couldn't tell how far the ball was going. And this was killing me.

So one day in January, about seven months after my accident, I couldn't stand it any longer and I told my dad that I just had to hit one outdoors. It was cold outside, probably below freezing, and there was snow piled up from a recent storm, but I didn't care. Dad found a relatively flat spot in the yard in front of the condo, shoveled the snow down to the grass, and pushed me into position. He hammered a spike into the frozen turf, tied a rope to it, and then attached the other end to my wheelchair, very much like we had done indoors. We did this to make sure that I would maintain my balance when I swung the club. The next step was to lift myself up from the seat so he could slide the pillow beneath me. I then tightened my waist strap and I was ready to hit my first shot outside after six months of agony.

To be sure, I was quite nervous. But I was also excited at the thought of what I was about to do. My nervousness over teeing-it-up was *very* different from what I felt before my accident. This was to be my new test, my own self-evaluation to see if I could ever hit a golf ball again. Ever so slowly, I took hold of my trusty 3-wood. It was a Byron Nelson model by MacGregor from the 1950s and it was a beautiful blonde piece of persimmon wood with a bright red and white insert. It was an earlier gift from my buddy Wayne, and I still have it today. The rough-textured cord grip felt a little uncomfortable in the cold and I was afraid I might lose my grip. So, I did what I used to do all of the time on the golf course: I spit into my golf glove and slowly gripped the club to try and get a more secure hold. My dad bent down gingerly and teed up a ball, got out of the way, and watched me take a pretty hard swing. The end result was not what I had hoped because I barely made contact, the ball traveling what seemed to be just a few yards. Man, did that make me mad! I knew I could do better. The next one I hit on the soleplate and it went about 100 yards. This was quite an improvement, but still not the shot I was looking for. My dad placed the third ball on the tee and this time I really nailed it. It went about 160 yards perfectly straight and I was absolutely thrilled. Dad was jumping up and down and we were high-fiving each other like two little kids who were just learning how to play the game. I had hit the ball right in the middle of the face of the club and it had felt *so* good. It was just amazing how much better I felt once I had that golf club in my hands and heard the smack of the ball.

In the months that followed I came to realize that as rotten as I felt everywhere else, whenever I went to the golf course I felt better. I knew in my heart and soul that golf was great physical *and* mental therapy for me. The more involved I was with golf, the more independent I felt. I always felt better sitting in my seat hitting golf balls than I did any other place. My thoughts now were beginning to focus on how I would support myself. I kept having a recurring nightmare from an old Humphrey Bogart movie where I was an old crippled man handing out towels in a fancy hotel bathroom or locker room somewhere. I was constantly worrying about how I was going to pay my bills and live on my own. For the time being I was fortunate to still be living at home without any expenses. It gave me time to be outside in the fresh air and explore a variety of possibilities. I briefly toyed with the idea of repairing golf clubs. I actually enjoyed doing it and wanted to learn more. A friend of mine had a golf repair shop and I thought that I would like to work there. The adventure lasted all of two days. As I sat there, I watched all those beautiful old golf clubs coming in for repairs and I couldn't stand it. I wanted to hit them, not work on them, so I quit my job. At the time, the thought of performing trick shots had not entered my mind. I often wonder what would have happened to me if I had pursued a career in golf club or watch repair.

– Chapter 8 –

Wayne Warms

I'VE BEEN LUCKY TO HAVE a few very close friends. One of them is Wayne Warms, who is actually more like a brother to me. Other than my family, Wayne has helped me more than anyone else. I frequently seek his advice on all kinds of things. Some are golf related issues, some aren't. He's a wise and compassionate person who often puts the interests of others ahead of his own. Wayne is also the consummate golf professional, with a high level of knowledge about the game and a healthy respect for its history and traditions. He's had an ongoing love affair with golf for as long as I have, and it was this great love that drew us together. That affection for the game, along with our respect and admiration for each other, is the foundation of our friendship.

Wayne and I grew up in the same place—Neptune, New Jersey—a small town in the central part of the state, not too far from the Atlantic Ocean. I'm four years older, though, so we never did anything together while we were growing up. I remember seeing him sometimes at Jumping Brook CC with his father, Don, but I really didn't have any contact with him. When I was 15, I stopped caddying at Jumping Brook and made the move over to Hollywood Golf Club. Wayne started caddying at "The Brook" not long after I left and soon became a fixture. In time, he went to work for Johnny Alberti in the golf shop. His golf game ultimately blossomed, too.

After high school, he went on to the University of Georgia and played on the Bulldog golf team.

Surprisingly, Wayne never had a real desire to play on the PGA Tour. He's one of the few people I know whose boyhood dream was to become a *club* professional rather than a *touring* professional. He loves to run tournaments and he's a gifted teacher. In my opinion, he's one of the finest instructors in all of golf. He has also been heavily involved in junior golf in New Jersey for many years and in 1995 won the National Junior Golf Leader Award from the PGA of America. His flair for merchandising is pretty impressive, too, and it's evident every time I go into his pro shop at Due Process Stable Golf Club in Colts Neck, New Jersey.

According to Wayne, he and I first met in June of 1969. I was trying to qualify for the New Jersey State Amateur at Manasquan River Golf Club in Brielle, New Jersey. Wayne was still working at The Brook, but he was at Manasquan that day watching a friend of his try to qualify. He knew me by reputation only, and was not quite sure if everything he heard about me was true or not. As far as my reputation back then, I plead guilty to having had a temper, although I have mellowed over the years. I remember breaking quite a few clubs and I also admit to a mischievous streak as well. My crowning achievement in the mischief department was hitting a ball through the halfway house window at The Brook just to see if it could be done.

The halfway house was a modest-sized A-frame building at the bottom of a hill, just to the right of the first fairway. I can't remember why I did it, but one evening I took dead aim at the "Frank Bank" hot dog machine and launched a low screamer that sailed right through the front window, setting off the burglar alarm. As dumb luck would have it, one of the members saw the whole thing and that set the wheels of justice in motion. As a result, I was temporarily banned from The Brook. After a while, I couldn't stand not being there so I would sneak onto the course to work on my game. I got caught again, and it resulted in an even longer suspension. I've often told Wayne that my behavior back then made it easy for him to look good in Mr. Alberti's eyes.

The first shot that Wayne ever saw me hit flew out-of-bounds on the 18th hole at Manasquan during my qualifying round for that state amateur. The ball sailed over a hedge and into the path of an oncoming car, almost causing a wreck. Due to what he had been told about my temper, he figured I would probably go nuts after snapping one out on the road. Instead, I calmly asked my caddie for another ball and rifled it down the fairway. I finished with a 74 to qualify easily. Our friendship began shortly thereafter.

I was starting college when Wayne was starting high school. During breaks from the University of North Texas, I would come home for short periods and occasionally play golf at Manasquan. At one point, Wayne left his job at The Brook and began working as the shop assistant for the head pro at Manasquan, John Cafone. "Mr. John," as we always called him, was the last of a dying breed of master club makers and he had a treasure trove of equipment above the pro shop. Wayne learned all the secrets about reshafting and refinishing clubs from Mr. John and he quickly became an expert in the field. Going to work at Manasquan may have been the biggest break of Wayne's career.

One day, Wayne showed me a driver that I thought was the most beautiful club I had ever seen. It was a dark, cherry-stained piece of persimmon wood with a red dot in the middle of the insert. The club was a MacGregor Toney Penna model from the 1950s and I begged Wayne to let me hit it. He finally gave in so we went to the 16th hole to try it out. Perfectly flat and straight, the 16th was an ideal place to test clubs. I had been thinking that I needed a club that would allow me to hit the ball on a lower trajectory, and this club did exactly that. Every shot rocketed down the fairway— low, long, and straight. I simply had to have that club and I finally managed to talk Wayne into giving it to me. I used that MacGregor driver right up until the time of my accident. A few years later, I gave it to my South African friend, Ed Holding.

Wayne visited me when I was in the hospital and made an effort to stay in touch while he was at the University of Georgia. When he graduated in 1975, he went to work full-time for Mr. John.

That summer I decided to start playing golf again but needed some help in figuring out how I could adapt my golf clubs to my new style of play. I called Wayne and asked him if he would help me begin my comeback and he agreed. I later found out that, initially, Wayne was extremely uncomfortable seeing me in my condition. As we began to work in earnest, however, his feelings quickly changed and he said that if I was willing to try and make a comeback, he would be at my side every step of the way. That unselfish commitment was a tremendous boost to me and it gave me an incentive to succeed.

(Let me say here that the initial discomfort that some people feel when they're in the presence of a disabled person is often very obvious. And it can be hurtful. This problem can best be overcome through education and positive interaction and, hopefully, I can be looked upon as a role model and an advocate to make public awareness grow in this area.)

As I mentioned, Mr. John was a genius at club making so the three of us spent the entire summer building a complete set for me. It took a lot of time, and there was much trial and error, but eventually I had a set of clubs that I could use. Actually, it was fun to experiment with various clubs to find out which would work best for me. Wayne and I decided that I could hit the ball better with longer clubs. Considering where I needed to position myself on the cart when I hit a shot, the extended length of the club eliminated the possibility of hitting the right rear fender on my backswing and downswing. A longer club also gave me more leverage, which would help me hit the ball farther. Graphite shafts were starting to come out at that time and because they were lighter than steel, we figured they would be perfect for me. A rep for Exxon Graphite Shafts named Pete Frasca very kindly gave me quite a few to use. Each and every day, Wayne and I experimented with different clubs and separated the ones that worked from those that didn't. The rejects went back to the laboratory above the golf shop.

In addition to trying out different clubs, we also experimented with different heads on different shafts. Since graphite was a precious commodity back then (and still is) Mr. John and Wayne had to come up with a creative way to remove the shafts from the club heads. They settled on a process that we called "graphite soup." We would bring a big pot of water to a boil, place a plastic bag over a club head, and then stick it into the pot. The high temperature would break the bond of epoxy that joined the shaft to the club head but without damaging either. By the end of the summer, after countless bowls of "soup," I had a custom set of clubs that fit me perfectly. I could now concentrate on fine-tuning my clubs, my swing, and my seat.

I hit golf balls all day long in search of the skill that I was just about desperate to develop. Learning to hit a ball while sitting down was virgin territory in golf instruction, so there wasn't a blueprint to guide me. At my side all of the way, giving me advice and encouragement, was Wayne.

Oddly enough, he told me many times that he gained a tremendous amount of information about the golf swing from watching me. Wayne still marvels at what I have accomplished:

"As a result of his paralysis, Dennis had to invent a new way to swing a golf club. His lower body was unable to function, therefore the use of hip turn, leg drive, and footwork was something that we could not use in the rebuilding of his swing. With tremendous concentration on his upper body movements, we had to make sure that his static fundamentals were correct. The first area we worked on was his grip. Before the accident, Dennis's left hand tended to be on the weak side or turned to the left. This was because of the tremendous lower body action, which would help him square the club at the point of impact. Without that lower body snap, Dennis had to rely more on his arms and hands to square the clubface at impact. We worked on a stronger left-hand position with the hand turned more to the right. After that we aligned his right hand to be parallel to his left, with particular attention paid to keeping the pressure in his two middle fingers. This positioning of his hands primed him for what would now have to be a monumental arm and hand release.

"Posture was also a critical factor in Dennis's relearning process. I found that because Dennis was strapped into his seat, his spine angle was more vertical. This allowed for a flatter swing plane that would incorporate a high amount of upper body torque. This torque would multiply the power to his hands and arms. To help increase his shoulder turn we moved the seat slightly to the right, creating a sort of preturned position. Next we had to work on how he parked his cart. With his seat turned to the right, the golf cart had to be parked slightly left of a normal alignment to offset his turned seat position. Finally, the correct ball position—which was also the bottom of his arc—had to be found. Surprisingly, we found it was in the same place as it had been before his accident. Dennis was able to find this point by visualizing a spot off his left breast instead of looking down at his feet. This spot is what I call his tangent point and finding it is crucial to him if he wants to play good golf.

"Now that this combination of preswing positioning had been worked out and adjusted for Dennis's new method of playing, it was time to focus on his actual swing. Dennis has always had unbelievable arm and hand speed. That's the reason he could hit the ball so far before his accident, even though his build was small in stature. He still has that speed. His swing is marvelous. When he hits the ball, his hands are down by his right leg while the club head appears to be over his head. That's how quick his hands are. He also has excellent hand-eye coordination and a great sense of feel for where the club head is. He is the ultimate hands and arms player.

"I believe Dennis proves that the body can be moved by a free flowing arm swing and that a significant amount of club head speed can still be generated despite a total absence of hip and leg movement. Dennis can still hit a golf ball a good 230 yards under normal conditions, a feat that I find remarkable. What you have to realize is that even though his legs are on the ground they are basically dead weight and useless while his upper body function is phenomenal. The two halves of Dennis's body are totally independent from each other. When you look at Dennis in this light, his accomplishments are even more impressive.

"The knowledge I have gained from working with Dennis has become the bedrock of my teaching philosophy. It reconfirms for me the importance of mastering preswing and in-swing fundamentals. Watching Dennis hit ball after ball, hour after hour, has given me an even greater appreciation of how the mind can will the body to do incredible feats. It has also given me immense pleasure seeing Dennis improve his ball striking technique over the years. In fact, I affectionately call him the human testing machine because he just doesn't miss many shots. I have never seen anyone who had to overcome more or anyone who worked harder than Dennis. It is said that positive events can grow out of negative circumstances. He totally personifies this. My heartfelt thanks to Dennis for all the times he educated me, motivated me, and above all inspired me."

Now that Wayne had helped rebuild my swing, it was at that point in my life that I was starting to prepare myself both physically and mentally to begin my comeback. With Mr. John's guidance and Wayne's help, I was able to gradually take small "steps" on the road back to my dreams. As I soon found out, however, it was to be a long and difficult journey.

– Chapter 9 –

The Mother of Invention

IT HAD BEEN ALMOST NINE MONTHS since my accident when I got a phone call from Jerry Volpe inviting me down to Florida. Jerry was one of the original investors with Ralph Terry at Roxiticus Golf Club, but now was living in Florida and was the owner of the Crystal Lago Country Club (now called Crystal Lake Country Club) in Pompano Beach. He told me that when I was feeling up to it he wanted me to come for a visit. I talked it over with my family and decided to make the trip. My dad and I flew down to Florida and planned to stay for just a week or two. However, we ended up staying for four months and what happened over the course of those months altered my life forever.

On one of my first days at Crystal Lago, I met Alec Ternyei. Alec was a golf professional from New Jersey and was a jack-of-all-trades around the golf course. He had a tremendous gift for visualizing and constructing things. Without a doubt he was one of the most talented individuals I have ever met. In his heyday, he was a fine player and a wonderful teacher. Alec was from the old school where he learned to play golf using hickory shafts and was the consummate arms and hands player. I knew this would have to be my style of play now so I was grateful to have him help me with my game. Alec had a move he called the "Hoboken Twist" whereby he accentuated his right arm crossing over his left through the impact area. I saw him teach this move to 70-year-old ladies and they would hit beautiful little right-to-left shots that would run like crazy when they hit the ground. Alec taught students to open the club on the back swing and close it on the way through.

I started hitting balls on the range at the club as soon as I arrived, and from day one Alec was there to help me. He watched as I set up for the first time and observed the procedure that I followed—the placement of my pillow, the strap and the anchor ropes for my wheelchair. Every day I would hit balls in the morning, take a break for lunch and then hit balls again in the afternoon. I got to where I could hit the ball about 180 yards with my driver, but I still couldn't play. Don't get me wrong, I was glad to be on the range, hitting bucket after bucket. But not being able to play was very frustrating. Finally, I couldn't stand it any longer and I asked Jerry's sons, John and Todd, if they would push me over to the first tee so I could play one hole. Alec went with us and as the Volpe brothers began to push me, I could feel my excitement building. When we got to the tee, I positioned myself so that I was aiming down the middle of the fairway and Alec pounded in the stakes for my wheelchair and tied the ropes securely in place. I lifted myself up and Alec put the pillow under me and I tightened my strap. I had the club in my hands and took a few practice swings. Then Alec teed up the ball for me. I took a swing and connected with the ball. It took off beautifully and landed down the fairway about 175 yards. The hole was 300 yards long so I was left with a shot of approximately 125 yards. Alec and the boys pulled up stakes and started pushing me down the fairway. Once we got to my ball, we had to go through the same routine of staking the chair down. When everything was set, I was ready for my next shot. I chose a 5-iron. Under the circumstances it was a decent shot that ended up about 10 feet to the right of the green. We again pulled up the stakes and headed toward the green. We then decided that I should use my putter and hit sitting sideways in my chair and eliminate the need for the time-consuming tie-down routine. I lined up my putt and stroked the ball to within a foot of the hole. I pushed myself onto the green and tapped the ball in for a par. Boy, did that feel great! Even par! To me, it was one of the best pars in the history of the game. Unfortunately, when I looked at my watch I saw that it had taken about 50 minutes to play one hole. I knew then that there had to be a better way for me to get around the golf course because I was bound and determined to play 18 holes again. Nothing was going to deny me my dream.

The next day I was sitting in the clubhouse recounting to everyone my miraculous par and moaning about the fact that at that pace it would take me a week to play 18 holes. Alec was there and saw me sitting on a barstool, swiveling back and forth. He kept looking at me and then I saw him scratch his head and heard him say, "Tomorrow when you come out to hit balls, you won't have the problem of getting around the golf course anymore."

Jerry had arranged for me to stay in a room that was downstairs next to the cart barn and I was awakened the next morning by the sounds of hammering and sawing. I slid out of bed into my wheelchair and opened my door to see what was going on. I looked out and saw the prettiest sight that I had ever seen. Alec had cut the legs off the barstool and mounted it on the passenger side of the cart. It was an early crude model of what was to become my lifeline to freedom, but to me it was beautiful.

Alec had taken the bench seat off the cart, which left the batteries exposed. On the passenger side he had made a frame and covered it with plywood, thus creating a base for the seat. He took the barstool, swivel and all, and mounted it to the base. He also attached three straps—one for my legs, one around my waist, and one to support my chest. With the stool mounted on the golf cart, Alec figured that I would be able to use the same technique to hit the ball as I did when sitting in my wheelchair, but now I had a way to quickly go from one shot to the next.

I couldn't wait to try it out. Alec helped transfer me from my wheelchair to the seat on the golf cart. Once I was settled I realized that—unlike with the wheelchair—the new seat moved around freely, which made it difficult for me to swing. Every time I took a swing (moving the club to the right) the seat moved to the left, which caused me to lose my balance. After I explained this to Alec, it took him all of two minutes to figure out how to solve the problem. He looked around and found a solid metal cylinder that was about eight inches long and about two inches in diameter. He picked it up, looked at it, then went over and drilled a hole in one end. He then inserted an ice pick in the hole to create a makeshift handle. I had no clue as to what he was doing, but thank goodness *he* did. Alec then drilled a two-inch hole in the seat and bolted the cylinder to the cart, just to the right of where the seat was when it was in the hitting position. I was beginning to get an idea of what Alec was trying to do and could see where it had a good chance of working.

I sat in the seat again and took hold of the ice pick and shoved the cylinder into the hole. Bingo! The seat was stable. It didn't move when I took a practice swing. I couldn't wait to try it out, so off to the range we went. I was now ready to hit a ball using this new technique. Hitting shots from the new seat was not that much different than hitting out of the wheelchair. I was up a little higher and actually felt better. I eventually took off the straps around my chest and legs and just used the one around my waist. I would hit balls on the range all morning and then venture out onto the course in the afternoon. The seat was in constant need of repairs and adjustments, but Alec was always there to help me. His invention was absolutely brilliant and all it needed was a little more refinement and I would be all set. Eventually, there would be two other generations of the seat and each one was better than the previous. The third production of the seat became an adjustable model. The seat remained steady on my backswing but through the use of a tension controlling device, it moved about three or four inches on my follow-through. This was an important change because now there was some give at the point of impact, whereas before there was none. I have hit thousands and thousands of shots from this seat and without this small amount of give I think I would have had some major back problems.

Another problem we encountered was the golf cart on which the seat was mounted. It was an old Cushman and had a big high fender that I had to avoid on my backswing. My backswing forced me to take the club outside, miss the fender, avoid the bag rack, and then do the same thing on the forward swing. I felt like I was a participant in an obstacle course. Although I now had the means to move about on the golf course freely, I was still frustrated because I was starting to see light at the end of the tunnel and just as I reached it the light would go out.

In 1976 my friend Gary Wiren was instrumental in setting up an appointment for me with E-Z-Go Golf Cart Company. He knew that I could hit the ball from the cart and thought that a different style cart might make it easier for me to swing the club. I met with the folks at E-Z-Go and they gave me a red, white, and blue cart that was far better than the one I was using. The fender on the new cart was much lower and the bag rack was no longer a problem. With these obstacles out of the way, my swing improved dramatically. I immediately added about 25 yards to my drives. E-Z-Go also helped in producing another seat. Frank Reese, who was employed by the company, looked at the seat that Alec had made and he took the mechanics of it and made it better. Frank was really impressed with the seat that Alec developed, but he wanted to fine-tune it so that if anything ever happened and it needed repair, even a novice could fix it. I owe a lot to Frank Reese and Alec Ternyei. In a real sense, they saved my life.

Chapter 10

Showman

THE EARLY YEARS were the toughest for all of us. I was trying to deal with my physical situation and I was not doing a great job handling the torment I was experiencing. Mentally, I was taking a beating and my family suffered as well. I'm sure it was not easy for them to see me like that day after day, and I'm sure that living in the same house with me had to be extremely difficult. On more than one occasion I took my frustrations out on them.

At that point it had been more than 18 months since the accident and I had virtually no idea of what I was going to do with the rest of my life. Any career in golf seemed so far in the distance that I could not imagine I would eventually become a performer. My parents knew, however, that I was always better off at the golf course than I was moping around the house. Basically, they let me do what I wanted. Hitting golf balls at that point, though, was simply an escape mechanism for me. Little did I know that this was a prelude to discovering a way to keep my dream alive.

I did know that I had to get my act together soon and, based on a few early shows (Newton Country Club in Jersey) and a couple of others, I decided to try and make a go of becoming a golf trick-shot artist and performer. I hung out my shingle so to speak, but it was a real struggle for the first few years to get any work.

The idea for a golf trick-shot career was formulated by memories from the mid-1960s when I was playing in the Metropolitan Junior Championship and Paul Hahn Sr., a world-class performer, did a show for all of the participants. It was great and I really enjoyed being in the audience. Even 10 years later I still remembered some of his shots and started to imitate what I had seen for my own show. At the time I saw his show I don't specifically remember saying that I would like to try any of his trick-shots. But because I remembered the show so vividly, there was no doubt that he definitely had a huge impact on me at the time.

Once I made the decision to go forward with my show, I made sure that any time a well-known golfer was giving a clinic near me, I'd try to attend. I went to see Sam Snead at Colony West Country Club in Fort Lauderdale. I thought that there would be hundreds, if not thousands, of people who would come to see him. Only about 40 people showed up and I was stunned. I'll never forget that. Today when I am doing my show, and I have a small crowd, I always think back to that clinic at Colony West. When we had a small crowd I would say to my dad, "Well, Sam Snead only drew 40 people, so I shouldn't feel bad." Through the years I have learned that it is so much harder to do a show in front of 40 people than it is to do it in front of 400 or 4,000 people. With a larger crowd it is easier because someone in the audience is bound to react to what you are doing or saying and that gets the crowd involved. That may not be the case with a small crowd. Crowd interaction is what makes a show successful. Any really good golfer can hit the shots I do, provided he or she practices a lot. But just hitting the shots does not make the show successful. I soon realized that what I was doing was also show business and your rapport with the audience and your presentation are what make for a really good show.

I also attended several wonderful clinics put on by golf legend Patty Berg. She encouraged me to keep trying and to always get the audience involved as much as possible. I took her advice then and I still continue to follow it. Whenever I see Patty I think back to my early years in show business and know that I was lucky to have her as one of my role models. Every year I get a Christmas card from her and it provides me with a lot of encouragement to know that she has followed my career all these years.

Another great golfer, Bob Toski, also was instrumental in helping me to get my show started in the right direction. I learned a lot about presentation, having a lot of energy, and being enthusiastic while doing a show. Another performer, Paul Buman, believed in using comedy but thought that it needed a purpose. He was very nice to me and I learned a few of my trick shots from him. He was great with the crowd and as I watched him, I was inspired to try to make a go of my golf show. Paul Hahn Jr. not only gave me valuable advice regarding trick shots, but he also gave me helpful information regarding the business aspect of setting up a show. He guided me when I was developing my first brochure and even sold me one of the sound systems that his dad had used in his show. Without the help and guidance and friendship of these people, I would have had a much more difficult time dealing with all of the hundreds of details and hurdles that I had to overcome in order to get my own show on the road.

In the summer of 1976 I actually did a few informal presentations, with the inaugural one coming at the Newton Country Club in New Jersey. Dick Howell was the professional and they held a benefit golf tournament in my honor. Dick found out that I had started to play golf again and asked me to come up to his club and show his members what I was working on. I thought this would be a wonderful way for me to thank the members for supporting the golf tournament and me. Dick's invitation also gave me a reason to practice and I discovered that I thoroughly enjoyed the workout. My show in the early years was called, "How to Play Golf Sitting Down." I demonstrated my new technique and tried to explain what was different and what was the same. I didn't have much of a script or a routine to follow, but I remember it was fun and the experience encouraged me to go forward. I also recall that there was a little pressure on me to come through when it counted but I found that it was the type of pressure that I liked and could handle.

In some ways, it brought back memories of the pressure I liked when I was playing competitively. When the audience applauded after I hit a good shot, I knew that the desire to succeed was in my blood. The seed was planted and I was on my way.

Up until then I had not done any trick shots. I was merely hitting the ball and letting the audience see what could be done from a sitting position. My first attempt at introducing a trick shot in my show came shortly after my visit to Newton Country Club. I remembered that Paul Hahn Sr. had hit a golf ball off of a three-foot high tee and I decided that this was going to be the shot that took my show into another phase. After a little practice, I was able to master the technique. I tried it in my show and got a much bigger reaction from the crowd than I could have ever anticipated. I was so encouraged by this that I contacted the PGA of America because I knew they had a film of Paul Hahn Sr. when he appeared at one of the PGA Championship's "Champions Clinic." I wanted to see if it was available and I wanted to study everything I could in order to improve my presentation. Although the PGA no longer includes a trick-shot artist at its clinic, I have tried for years to get them to reinstate this tradition. I believe that the audience would benefit from this and give them the experience of seeing professional golf from another point of view. I also studied a book by one of golf's first trick-shot artists, Joe Kirkwood. I soaked up the information from these two masters like a sponge. The shots I learned from these two experts became the foundation of the beginnings of my future show. As time went by, I started to gain more confidence and began to experiment by making up my own shots and routines.

Dr. Gary Wiren was the national education director for the PGA of America and he soon became an important mentor to me. He is one of the absolute best speakers you will ever hear and his help and encouragement went a long way toward building the foundation of my budding career. He was the person most responsible for setting up the sequence of events that led me to getting my first golf cart from E-Z-Go, but he also arranged for me to do my first major exhibition. In 1977, the PGA Merchandise Show was held at Disney World behind the Contemporary Hotel where Bob Toski, Jim Flick, and I put on a demonstration. My portion lasted about 20 minutes and again I focused on how to play golf sitting down. I hit ball after ball into the lake, which was our target area. The only trick shot that I hit that day was the one using my three-foot tee. The one thing that really stands out in my mind about that appearance was that the Titleist rep came by and gave us a gross of Titleist golf balls to use. Bob Toski and I had a contest to see who could make the ball skip the most times across the lake. He won with seven skips but I was close with six.

At the end of the show the Titleist rep came over to congratulate me. "There are nine balls left from the gross." He added, "Do you want to keep them?"

"If I knew you were going to let me keep what was left," I replied, "I never would have hit that many into the lake."

Today, Gary Wiren is a world-renowned instructor, lecturer, and successful businessman. I will never forget his kindness and friendship. He still tries to downplay what he did for me, but I know I would not be where I am without his help. Gary, recalling those early years, says, "Helping Dennis was all in the name of friendship. I was so impressed with his story and his message was so important and inspirational that I wanted to help him reach as many people as possible. You've got people out there who come up with these little excuses about why they can't do this and why they can't do that and then there's Dennis, showing them that they can do it if they want it badly enough. We have been friends for a long time and that is what friends do for each other.

"Dennis has the tenacity, he has the passion, and he was bound and determined he was going to make it whether it was on the PGA Tour or the South African Tour or the Dennis Walters Golf Show Tour. He truly loves golf. He is one of the straightest, most consistent drivers of the ball that I have ever seen. The shape of his shots and the trajectory are things that are just automatic for him. I have witnessed him go on his long journey towards becoming a true professional in every sense of the word and I am very proud of him.

"I am a strong advocate of proven fundamentals in the golf swing and I use Dennis as an example in my presentation on the importance of a proper address. He has to park his cart in the right place and then he has to set himself up in the seat in just the right way. The fundamental here is aiming and just to prove my point, I usually take out a folding chair and show the audience how Dennis would sit in the chair. Then I point the chair a little to the right and ask what they would have to do in order to hit the ball at the target. This is a great visual example of alignment. Dennis will tell you that the most important thing for him when he parks his cart is to have it pointing in the right direction. I think that it is easy to lose sight of the most basic ingredients of a good golf swing and I use Dennis to remind the audience of this."

After that appearance at the PGA Show, and with Gary's help, I got a few bookings. Most of the time, though, it was really tough trying to find work. My dad was my biggest fan and knew that this was something that would give me a new lease on life. He made hundreds of phone calls and never gave up trying to get me a show. I remember his excitement every time he got a live one. He would say, "Hot damn, I just booked one." In the meantime, while my dad was busy with his phone calls, I continued to practice my regular swing and to perfect new trick shots. I also worked on my oral presentation because I felt that it was a key way to connect with the audience. I spoke about how golf was always my dream and that it looked like the dream was going to be taken away from me after my accident. My message was that with hard work and perseverance, you can achieve your dreams and be successful at almost anything.

I made sure to stress this theme throughout my show. I tape-recorded my practice sessions as well as my shows and I had Gary critique them. I hadn't had any training as a public speaker and definitely needed some advice. Actually, I think I worked as hard on my speaking skills as I did on my golf swing. Gradually, with Gary's help, I began to improve. I also found out that I was starting to enjoy speaking in front of people and that I had the ability to ad lib and think fast on my feet. My dad used to say that I had "the natural gift of a great bull-shitter."

I knew I had a good story to tell and I was gratified when an audience let me know that they appreciated my golf skills and my humor. People were very receptive to my positive message. I just tried to be honest and genuine. I think people look for ways to be motivated and inspired and I hoped I could do this for them. Motivation should come from within, but it is good to have someone help to bring it to the surface.

After I started my golf show in 1977 my dad had to make hundreds of calls just to book a few shows. By some miracle, my dad was able to schedule 10 shows that first year. I would have had 11 events, but we had to turn one down because of a logistics problem. That really upset me because I wanted to be as busy as I could. My dad and I were so naïve that we thought it was a fluke occurrence and that a scheduling problem like that would never happen again. The show that I had to turn down was scheduled to be in Chicago, which normally would not have been a problem. Unfortunately, though, I was going to be in New Jersey the day before the Chicago show and there was just no way that we could drive to Chicago in time. Later that same year we were asked to do a clinic in Puerto Rico and ran into the same problem. There wasn't any way to get my golf cart there in time, and without my swivel seat I couldn't do the show.

It seemed that every time I managed to get over one hurdle in my life, another one would pop up. Dad, who could solve almost any problem, thought of the perfect solution to the trouble we kept having. Instead of having to deal with how to get my golf cart somewhere, he decided that we should make a seat that we could take on an airplane and mount on a golf cart wherever we were giving a show. It was a brilliant idea and it opened up a whole new world for me. I called Frank Reese at E-Z-Go and asked him if Dad's idea was possible. He said sure, then made us another base. The barstool seat that I was using would have been too big to fit in a travel case so my cousin Nino made a smaller seat out of aluminum that folds up. We then had two travel cases made—one for the portable base and one for the portable seat. From that point on, "The Dennis Walters Golf Show" became more mobile.

For the next several years, the learning process continued. My skills improved, but I began to get really discouraged because my number of bookings was still not enough to keep me busy full-time. I don't think I ever really thought of quitting, but I did come close several times. Gary Wiren had a good friend, Sam Hakemian, who was a very successful insurance executive. Sam, an avid golfer and a man with a kind heart, heard about my struggles from Gary and he jumped on the bandwagon in a big way. Sam sponsored me for several years and underwrote my appearances at 10 to 15 events a year. Gary, Sam, and I would decide where the shows would take place and usually we picked junior golf events or charity tournaments. The events we chose would not have a budget to bring in someone to do a show and so they were happy to have me add an extra dimension to the event. It was great for me because I had the opportunity to gain more exposure and it also gave me the chance to see which of my routines worked and which ones didn't. Every time I did a show I knew that the coverage I was getting would lead to what my dad called "spin-offs"—another booking that we got as a result of a show we did. Sam made it possible for me to continue the pursuit of my dreams. Along the way, he also became a cherished friend.

Up to this point my only sponsorship had been with Sam. My first actual golf sponsorship was with PGA Victor, which provided me with golf equipment. Later Joe Phillips from Wilson signed me to a contract not only for equipment, but also included a few thousand dollars to boot. At about the same time I was introduced to Vince Draddy of Izod and he was nice enough to give me $1,000 and all the shirts I needed. I loved those shirts because they had huge alligators on them and were available only to tour players. I was finally beginning to see some progress, but it still wasn't happening fast enough for me.

As my struggles continued, little did I know that I was about to receive one of the most important breaks of my career. My dad, unbeknownst to me, wrote a very personal and emotional letter to Jack Nicklaus. At the time, Jack was the majority owner of MacGregor Golf. My dad knew that Jack had five children so he tried to appeal to him as a father. My dad got a letter back from Jack that promised that George Nichols, the president of MacGregor, would be getting in touch with me. Not long after that George called and invited us to visit the MacGregor headquarters in Albany, Georgia. We were elated. We went to Albany and got a tour of the factory, then went to Doublegate Country Club where I showed the MacGregor people how I hit balls. I also told them what I was trying to do with my show and outlined my goals for the future.

Before we left, Mr. Nichols said that MacGregor wanted to sponsor me and that they would pay me $25,000. I couldn't believe it. I felt as if I had won the lottery. To make the deal even sweeter for me was the fact that I had been using some of their clubs for a long time and MacGregor's were always my favorite. It was just too good to be true. As a result of this sponsorship I was able to select the best persimmon heads and have all of my clubs custom-made. In addition, MacGregor was instrumental in producing my first professionally-done brochure, poster, and promotional video. Everyone we met at MacGregor was just great. Thanks to the great Jack Nicklaus opening the door for me, I now had a well-respected company and its total sales force helping me promote my show. I made many appearances around the country for MacGregor and kept getting those spin-offs that I loved. After a year or two I had worked my way up to doing about 75 shows a year and for the first time definitely considered myself to be a full-time professional golfer. I will always be indebted to Jack for helping me realize my dream and will be forever grateful for the faith that he had in me. That's why it means so much to me to have had him write the foreword for this book.

The early years in business were filled with a lot of sorrow and frustration and hopes of chasing my new dream. The encouragement of my family and friends was so crucial to me. And while I almost called it quits several times, the strength that I gained from their love, along with my own inner desire, kept me going. I was able to follow the advice that I gave to every audience: never give up. For the first time since the accident, I really felt that my perseverance and hard work was finally paying off.

*   *   *

By the way, a couple of years after I was discharged from the Kessler Institute, I got my chance to fulfill the promise I had made to the doctor who told me I'd never play golf again. It turned out to be one of the most pleasurable moments I've had since my accident. By then, I had my special golf cart with its swivel seat, and a trailer that I pulled behind my van. We had also adapted the trailer so that I could get the cart on and off by myself. So, on a beautiful, crisp morning, I drove up to Kessler, took the cart off the trailer, set everything up and began to hit golf balls into the Essex County West Country Club grounds across the street. I hadn't told anyone in advance that I was going to do this, and before I knew it patients were hanging out of windows and doorways cheering loudly for me. The sensations this reaction created for me gave me a great sense of pride and accomplishment, something that I had been missing since that fateful July day.

Apparently, someone at the hospital called a local TV station and a newspaper because it wasn't long before some reporters arrived on the scene. The doctor who had told me that I'd never play golf again was there, too, watching me with awe. Eventually, he walked over to me, shook my hand, and told me how happy he was that he had been proven wrong. He also told me that he would never again crush another person's dreams.

Because of what I did that day, I'm sure that encouraging others to reach for their dreams became the foundation of my show and the hallmark of my life.

– *Chapter 11* –

Muffin

WHEN I WAS A BOY, our family had a dog named Taffy. She was a cocker spaniel mix and very sweet natured. My mom and dad had gone to Atlantic City for a few days and decided to surprise my sister Barbara and me with a puppy. Before they came home they went to an animal shelter and found a dog they liked. Since Atlantic City is famous for its salt-water taffy, that's where the dog's name came from. Back in those days, shelters did not automatically neuter or spay animals before they were adopted, so my parents were able to pick one out and get her right away. All my dogs since that first one have come from shelters. I believe that anyone who is looking for a dog or cat should begin his or her search at a local humane society or animal shelter. There are so many wonderful animals at these places and they are in desperate need of good homes. Save one of these creatures and you'll find that it will turn out to be one of the best things you will ever do.

Taffy came to live with us when I was about two years old. When I started kindergarten I hated to leave her and couldn't wait to get home to play with her after school. During the years she lived with us she had three litters of puppies. One time I came home from school and she was giving birth in the garage. This was quite startling and amazing for a 10-year-old to witness. After the puppies were a few weeks old, Barbara and I began playing with them in the front yard. There were many fun moments where we simply rolled around on the grass and they would come up, lick us in the face, and just enjoy all the love and attention we could give them. That always made it hard for us to part with the puppies, but we were fortunate to always find them good homes and, besides, we still had Taffy after the puppies were gone. Taffy lived with us for 15 years and I still have her original rabies tag. I have put that tag on the collars of every dog that I have had since her, just to let each of them know that they had big boots to fill.

When I went away to college I used to pet every dog I saw and wished that I had one of my own. After my accident I was in a daze for a long time. On many occasions I was so depressed that I wouldn't even get out of bed for days. Finally, in 1977, I decided that I needed a companion and that I should look for a nice dog like Taffy. I began my search by looking in the local newspaper and found an advertisement for an animal rescue group. I went down to the shelter with high hopes, certain that this would be the cure for my blues. I was on my crutches because I rarely went out in public in a wheelchair in those days. I struggled down each row of cages until I found an adorable dog that I liked right away. However, even though the dog would be mine, I felt that the choice should be a family decision. To be fair, I wanted my mom and dad to see the dog before I actually brought it home. So I asked the lady in charge if she would hold the dog for me with the provision that I would be back shortly with my family.

I had not been this happy or had not looked forward to something as exciting as this in a very long time and couldn't wait to get back to the shelter. When my parents and I arrived back there a few hours later, the same lady I had talked to earlier was still there.

"I'm here to pick up my dog," I said. Her response just about knocked me over.

"I'm sorry, but that dog has already been adopted."

I couldn't believe it and became almost frantic. As fast as I could, I hurried up and down each row looking for another dog. I finally found another one that I liked and pointed her out to the lady. "I'll take that one."

Again, luck was nowhere to be found. The lady told me that that dog had also been adopted. But I was determined and found yet a third one. My dad went to get the lady but came back alone. "She says that one is spoken for, too."

Hearing that really ticked me off, so I went to find her. "What's the deal here?" I asked her. "Is every dog in this place adopted?"

She obviously didn't like this. "You could never take care of a dog," she said. "Who's going to take it out for a walk? I'm just not letting you have a dog. There is no way that someone in your condition could take care of a pet."

I was shattered and I wanted to scream at her and cry at the same time. It was the first but, unfortunately, not the last example of discrimination due to my condition that I would experience. I was so dumbfounded that I couldn't even respond to that woman. I was sure that I could take as good care of a dog—legs or no legs—as anyone. We left, and I decided that I would go to the Broward County Humane Society the next day and look for a dog. Today, thanks to the generosity of Wayne and Marti Huizenga, the BCHS is a state-of-the-art facility. Back then it was just a cramped little building with a lot of dogs and cats. I met the kennel manager, Joanne Roman, and I told her that I really wanted a dog. I assured her that my pet would have a great home, be well taken care of, and be smothered with love. She never looked at me as a person with a disability. She looked at me as a person who would be a wonderful pet owner. She had absolutely no reservations and suggested that I find a dog that was between two and four years old because they would be mature. I told her that I wanted a female that was small, but not tiny, and weighed about 15 pounds. I then looked at all the dogs but didn't see one that I felt was perfect. Joanne then told me that all the new dogs that came to the facility were put on display each Wednesday morning at 10 o'clock. So, for the next several weeks I made it a point to be there early. Unfortunately, I was not successful. Joanne, however, encouraged me not to give up looking.

A while later, my friend Wayne happened to be visiting me one Wednesday. When I told him about my dog search, he said he would go with me to see if there were any new ones.

When we got there, Wayne started his search on one end of the kennel while I started on the other. At one point, Wayne shouted, "Hey Dennis! I found a really cool dog. It's a female, she's the right size, and she is very friendly. She kissed my hand and wanted me to play with her."

Without seeing her, I went to find Joanne. But before I could tell her about Wayne's discovery, she said, "Dennis, I think I have just the right dog for you." I told her that Wayne had found one, too, but she said she wanted me to see the one that she had her eye on before I made a decision. Wayne and I went into her office and the anticipation was almost unbearable. It seemed to take forever, but finally Joanne came in with this beautiful brown and white dog that appeared to be a mixed breed cocker spaniel. She was white with butterscotch ears and four butterscotch splotches on her back. Wayne smiled and said, "That's the same dog I found."

By now, I was beside myself. Joanne put the little dog down on the floor and I asked, "Does she have a name?"

"This is Muffin," Joanne replied.

I called her name and she came right over to me, jumped in my lap and started licking my face. I couldn't stop smiling and hadn't felt that happy in a long time. It turned out that Muffin was two years old. She had short legs, but she had the body of a bigger dog. She was solid and weighed about 14 pounds. I knew that she just had to come home with me and because she had already been spayed, I was able to take her home that day. Joanne gave me a leash and a collar and some food to get me started, and told me that Muffin might be a little scared and timid at first because she would be in new surroundings. However, that never happened. From the first day, Muffin fit right in. She actually fell asleep in my arms as Wayne drove me home. I had really lucked out with this dog. She was well-mannered and housebroken and I was just thrilled to have a loyal pet to take care of. I now had something to get me going every morning and keep me busy all day.

My parents and I were living in a garden apartment right off the 14th tee on the West Course at Jacaranda Country Club, a place I have called home for the past 26 years. The apartment was on the ground floor and had a large terrace. I kept my golf cart on the terrace and knew that even though I couldn't run with Muffin, I could still give her plenty of exercise. I figured that I would let her run alongside the golf cart on the golf course. I bought a leash about 30 feet long so that Muffy could run comfortably away from the cart. The first three days I had her, we created a loop on the golf course. We went down the 14th hole, up the 15th, across the 16th and back to the 12th. My reasoning for doing this was that I thought if Muffin ever accidentally got out of the house, she would run the loop and end up back home.

For three days I ran Muffy on this loop and she was doing great and seemed to be really happy to be with me. On the fourth day, I was taking an afternoon nap because it was raining. I woke up and couldn't find Muffin. I called her but she did not come into my room. I got into my wheelchair and went out to the living room to see what mischief she could be in. I did not see her, but I still was not that concerned. Then I noticed that the sliding glass door was open and I figured Muffy had gotten out and had run away. As fast as I could, I got into my golf cart and headed out for our loop. I was going as quickly as I could, and was fighting to keep the tears back at the same time. The only thought going through my mind was that I had finally found a great dog and now I had lost her. I looked everywhere and couldn't find her. I decided I would drive home and get someone to help me. As I pulled the cart onto the terrace, I saw Muffin sitting on the porch of the condo next door. She had probably been sitting there the entire time, but in my hurry to get out and find her, I passed right by her. I can't tell you how long it took for my heart to settle back to a normal beat. I was just so happy to see her, and believe me, she knew it. Our bond was forever sealed.

I usually played golf about five days out of the week and many of those days I played with my friend Steve Magula. Steve and his brothers, Gus and Mike, had been well-known athletes in Pennsylvania and they even had their own traveling semipro basketball team, the Vagabond Kings. Steve would bring his dog Lucky out to the golf course and Lucky and Muffin became friends. Lucky was black with a beautiful rooster-like tail, while Muffin was white and butterscotch with a white rooster-like tail. Although they were the same size and shape, they made quite a contrast and everyone at the golf course knew and loved them.

Muffin and I also befriended some Muscovy ducks at Jacaranda. We used to see them every day during our run. One time we spotted a mother duck being followed by a dozen baby ducks. Two of the babies were all yellow, which meant they would be white when full grown. I started bringing bread with us to feed the ducks and since the two yellow ones had become my favorites I made sure that they got plenty. I was concerned about all the babies because, being so little, they were easy targets for predators. The bigger the ducks got, the more bread I went through daily. One day my mom mentioned that we had been going through an awful lot of bread. I just told her that I was a growing boy and was eating a lot of sandwiches. When the two yellow ducks were full-grown they were all white except that each one had a black spot on its head. I nicknamed them the Black Hat Brothers.

Muffin and I really enjoyed seeing those ducks. My golf cart was the only red one at Jacaranda and before long the ducks could easily recognize it. Even if they were two fairways away, once they saw me they would run as fast as they could to my cart. The two Black Hat Brothers would jump right into the cart and sit beside Muffin. They became an unlikely trio. We saw the Black Hat Brothers for many months and then one day, when I went out to feed them, they never appeared. I often wondered what happened to them and decided that they must have joined a different golf club. Muffin and I dearly missed our feathery friends.

To make it easier for me to walk Muffin when I was using my crutches, I bought a 30-foot retractable leash. On a trip to Memphis, Tennessee, once, we were staying on the second floor of a hotel. At one point I had to meet my dad in the lobby so Muffin and I rode down on the elevator. As I stepped out, one crutch got caught on something and I stumbled and lost my balance for a moment. I didn't fall down and I managed to hold onto Muffin's leash, but, on the other hand, I also couldn't do anything to stop the elevator doors when they started to close—with Muffin still inside. Picture that if you can. Me on the outside of the elevator with the leash in my hand, Muffin still attached to the leash, inside the elevator, and it started to go up. Now picture that retractable leash playing out like a fishing reel and line. When the elevator stopped on the second floor, I was terrified that it would continue up. If it had, Muffin probably would've been strangled. Totally helpless at this point, all I could do was pray that the elevator would return to the ground floor. Luckily for both of us, it did. And when the doors opened, there was little Muffin sitting in the same spot as if nothing had happened. I was just about having a heart attack and she was calmly sitting there, waiting for me to tell her to come on. If dogs could talk, I'm sure she would have said something like, "You need to learn how to relax, my friend. You humans are much too dramatic." I will never forget the close call we had that day.

Muffin was such a good traveler and so quiet when she was on an airplane that sometimes we just didn't bother to tell the airline that she was with us. If we could get away with it, it would save us 50 dollars per trip. For most flights there was a limit of one pet in coach and one pet in first class. On one trip, Dad and I had preboarded and were sitting in the coach section. As the other passengers began coming down the aisle, we noticed a woman with a pet carrier. We figured she had a reservation for her dog, so we were sure we'd get kicked off the plane if we got caught with our stowaway. Once everybody got onboard, however, we thought we'd made it. But just as the door of the plane was about to be closed, a gate agent came on and headed straight toward us. Clearly, she was going to escort us off the plane. Instead, she pointed a finger at Dad and me and said, "You two can move to first class, if you'd like." And with a smile, she added, "Your dog, too." Later, our flight attendant told us that the gate agent was a dog lover and had known all along that I had smuggled Muffin on board.

Another time we were in Birmingham, Alabama, to take part in the golf tournament that Charlie Boswell put on every year. Charlie was perhaps the most famous blind golfer of all time. One of the celebrity participants in the event was Bob Hope, who, it turned out, was staying at the same hotel as we were. One night, Dad and I took Muffin out for a walk and came upon a woman who was walking two dogs. Naturally, Muffin started barking at them.

"Do you know who your dog is barking at?" the lady asked rather indignantly.

"No, we do not," I said.

"These are Bob Hope's dogs," she sniffed, "and I am the dog walker. You might say I am their nanny."

With that my dad said, "This is Muffin, he's Dennis, and I'm Bucky. This is a low-budget operation. We walk our own dog."

Sometimes our trips went smoothly, sometimes they didn't. One year we were asked to do a show in Gallup, New Mexico. When we made our reservations, we learned that we would have to first fly to Albuquerque and then take a small commuter plane to Gallup. We also discovered that the small commuter plane was not pressurized and so Muffin would not be able to get on the plane. Our alternate arrangements included getting a truck to carry the equipment as well as Muffin.

Well . . . it was only about 120 miles between Albuquerque and Gallup, but it turned out to be one of the worst flights that I have ever experienced. We had hardly gotten off the runway when we flew into a bad storm. Turbulence, thunder, lightning—you name it. The airplane was bouncing all over the place and we were getting tossed around like rag dolls. Some of the passengers were saying "Hail Marys" and turning green. My dad, though, who could nap through anything, had fallen asleep before we had even taken off and he slept through the entire rough ride. As we got up over some mountains, and the turbulence subsided, he suddenly woke up, stretched and said, "What a great flight!" Several of the passengers, including me, started throwing things at him. Two hours after we landed, Muffin arrived and seemed none the worse for her first trip without me. Had I known beforehand that we were going to be taking the "Flight from Hell," I definitely would have opted to ride in the truck with Muffin and our equipment.

We always took Muffin on our trips but often had to sneak her into our hotel in a pet carrier called a Sherpa. One place we stayed at frequently was the Marriott Courtyard in New York. When we stayed there, Dad would put Muffin in the bag and sneak her out for a last walk around 10 p.m. After watching Dad go out at the same time for several nights in a row, the hotel manager finally asked him what was in the bag. Thinking quickly, Dad replied, "I don't like to leave cash in the room when I am not there, so I take it with me."

The manager chuckled and said, "Well, your money has two eyes and a tail."

As he usually did in these situations, Dad managed to talk his way out of trouble. The manager then told him that some Marriott hotels made exceptions for people traveling with pets, but that it was up to each hotel. I knew that we would soon be moving to another Marriott so I took a chance and called ahead to see if we could bring Muffin with us legally instead of sneaking her in.

The manager replied, "If they are small and well-behaved pets, we do allow it. May I have your name, and have you ever stayed here?"

"My name is Dennis Walters," I said, "and yes, I have."

"Oh, hi, Mr. Walters. We've been wondering how long it would take you to tell us that you had a dog with you."

From that point on, Muffin walked into that hotel right alongside me. The management became so impressed with her behavior that they even wrote a letter of reference for us to present at other Courtyard Hotels so that they, too, would let Muffin stay as a guest.

*　　*　　*

I never taught Muffin any tricks, so she never did anything during my shows except sleep, which she did with a lot of class. She was certainly a lady. Having a dog that did tricks was not the reason I wanted one. Muffin's job was to lift up my spirits and keep me company. Period. That's why she was the perfect dog for me. I gave her unconditional love and she gave it back to me. Whether at practice or during a show, Muffin would sleep on the driver's seat of the golf cart. Amazingly, she always woke up at the same point in my performance. It was right when I was about to hit my second to last trick shot, which I called the "Fire Shot." Somehow, she knew my routine—even in her sleep—and knew when there were only two shots left. I don't know how she knew this, but she just did.

Muffin was also unusual in the fact that she never barked at people. Only when she saw another dog would she bark. Seriously, sometimes she would go three or four weeks without making a sound and I would start to worry that she had forgotten how. When my dad and I would take her for a walk, we'd make a point to try and find another dog just so we could hear her bark.

Another great thing about Muffin was that she was kind of a social icebreaker for me. After I had my accident, I soon realized that many people weren't comfortable being in the company of someone in a wheelchair. When Muffin was on my lap, however, people were much more inclined to come over and talk. That interaction, I have no doubt, was largely due to Muffin. Today, thankfully, with so much emphasis being placed on trying to find a cure for paralysis, attitudes have changed for the better and more and more people are comfortable being around those of us who are physically challenged.

In 1989 I was scheduled to do my show at the Canadian Open. While we were there a lady came up to us and wanted to know if Muffin was a puppy because she looked so healthy. Unfortunately, she looked good on the outside but things were not so good on the inside. Muffin got sick during that trip so we took her to a local vet who told us that she had a kidney problem. The vet was a very kind lady who said she would try to treat Muffin, but it really did not look too good. We stayed in Canada for a few more days while the vet was taking care of Muffin in the hospital. Her condition worsened and my dad and I were beside ourselves. One afternoon when I returned to the hotel after visiting Muffin, I knew what had to be done. I told my dad that we were not doing this for Muffin, but that we were keeping her alive for us. I called home and spoke to my mom and Barbara and told them that Muffin was not going to make it and that I had decided that it was best for Muffin if we ended her suffering. Once I reached that conclusion, I knew putting her to sleep would be the right thing. I called the vet with my decision and she told us to come back after office hours when no one else would be there. My dad and I went in and held Muffin and we talked about all the wonderful times we had together. The vet let us stay and I held Muffin for an hour. I laughed and I cried but it was good for both of us. When it was time to have the procedure, I held her in my arms and said goodbye to her and the doctor gave her the injection. It was over instantly. My dad, who was as tough as they come, let out the loudest bloodcurdling scream I had ever heard. We brought her ashes back with us and she is buried under a palm tree in our backyard. Barbara, knowing how much Muffin liked to play with squirrels, found a ceramic squirrel that now stands guard over her grave.

I had Muffin for about 12 years. She was a wonderful dog, and I truly believe that she helped save my life and sanity during that dark, dark period. She made it much easier for me to hang in there when there were difficult times.

Fortunately, Muffin had her photo taken with every famous person we met, including Arnold Palmer, Jack Nicklaus, Miss America, Ben Hogan, and former President George Bush. My memories of her are part of my scrapbook collection and they provide me with many happy moments. Since Muffin, I've had two other dogs. But I still miss her and not a day goes by that I don't recall something fun that we did together.

– Chapter 12 –

Mulligan

AFTER MUFFIN DIED, my dad and I went on a search for another dog. In every town we went to across America, we would go to the local humane society or dog pound to see if the pooch that I was looking for was there. The routine was always the same: we would get into town and go directly to the golf course and check it out in advance of the show. After we made sure that everything was in order, we would then head over to the local animal shelter. Muffin had passed away in early September and since my tour would not end until mid-November, we still had about six weeks of travel left and I was sure that I would be able to find a dog in that time. I came close a few times, but none of them were absolutely what I was looking for. So, by the time I returned home I was still without a new dog and it felt as if I were missing part of my soul.

I took a few days off and tried to unwind but couldn't relax because all I could think about was getting another dog. Finally, I called my friend Joanne Roman at the Broward County Humane Society and enlisted her help. She said they were in the process of building a new facility and weren't taking in many dogs at that time. She would, however, keep her eye out for one. She remembered that I had gotten Muffin there and was aware of the kind of dog that I was looking for. Because of the new construction, my chances of finding a dog there were slim but the end result was a fabulous, state-of-the-art facility that is now considered one of the foremost humane society structures in the country. It's called the Marti Huizenga Humane Society of Broward County, and I'm proud to say that it contains the Muffin Adoption Room where people can get to know the pets they are planning to take home with them.

After alerting Joanne about my search for a new dog, I found an additional source—a network of elderly ladies in the Fort Lauderdale area who were dedicating their time to finding homes for wayward dogs. I contacted them, explained my situation, and described the kind of dog I was looking for. They were simply great, and they made it their mission to find the right one for me. I then began to get calls from them day and night asking me to go to various locations to see the dogs that they had found. This process went on for weeks and, unfortunately, without success. My days were feeling more and more empty. I was used to having Muffin beside me all of the time and I missed having a companion.

Before I knew it, it was January and time for the PGA Merchandise Show in Orlando. We had been going to the show for several years (it was a great place to see old friends, make new contacts, and hopefully get a few bookings) and Muffin had always gone with us. She would sit on my lap all day long and people would be drawn to her. This particular year, part of me did not want to go because a lot of people did not know that Muffin had passed away and I was afraid that I would start to cry if someone asked me where she was. But I went anyway.

Since the previous September we had visited the Orlando Humane Society several times, although without any luck. But since we would be going past the facility on our way to the convention center, I told my dad that we might as well stop and take a peek. "We don't have anything to lose, plus we're way ahead of schedule."

When we drove into the parking lot of the Humane Society, I immediately had a feeling that something good was going to happen this time. To this day, I still don't know why.

The facility was set up with the small dogs in the back—and I mean *way* back. On crutches, it seemed to take forever. We arrived at the first row of cages and there were some cute dogs but none of them caught my eye. I was a bit dejected by this, but my dad said there were a few more dogs farther down. At the very last cage, we saw that there were two inside. I looked at the card with the description of the smaller of the two and couldn't believe what I read. It said that the dog was two years old, female, good with children, and housebroken. I started to feel my heart pound and was trying not to get too excited. I asked my dad to go get one of the volunteers so I could get a closer look.

While I was waiting for someone to come back I bent over and stuck my hand in the cage to pet her. She started to lick my hand and I knew I had hit the jackpot. When the volunteer arrived, I handed her the card and said I wanted to see the small one. She opened the cage, picked up the bigger dog and started to hand it to me. I said, "No, no, I'm interested in the small dog." The volunteer said that the card I had handed her was for the other dog. I said, "Okay, I was wrong. I still want to see the small one."

I only had eyes for the little gray fluffball that was still licking my hand. Unfortunately, when I read the correct card it said the dog was female, six months old, but not housebroken. The volunteer then said, "I don't think you want this dog. She's been biting everybody since she got here."

I heard her but it didn't matter, because I could feel it in my bones that my search was very close to being over. She brought the dog out and I said that I wanted to sit down on one of the benches and hold her. While I petted her, she continued to lick my hands and face. Suddenly, she jumped from my lap and took off. About 10 seconds later she came around the corner again as fast as she could, her paws sliding on the linoleum floor as she tried to make the turn. She made it to the bench finally, then jumped up and put her head on my knee. At that exact moment, I recalled what a lady from my Fort Lauderdale network had once told me: "It may take awhile, but when you find the right one, you'll know it and feel it instantly." I believed her.

Over the previous weeks, I had done some research and learned that there were certain personality traits to look for when choosing a dog. The first test was to find out if she trusted me. The way I did this was by cradling the dog on her back to see if she would relax and not squirm. She did great, so I was sure she felt safe with me. Since I was prone to dropping my crutches on the floor after I would sit down—which could make a loud noise—I needed to make sure that she wouldn't be too scared or skittish when it happened. The little gal passed this test with flying colors, too. Finally, I needed to see how she interacted with other dogs and in a crowd of people. I asked the volunteer to bring out some more dogs and then sent my dad to see if he could round up a few of the other volunteers. With the other dogs running around barking and with several people standing there, my little jewel just behaved beautifully. Sitting there watching her, it felt as if a fog had been lifted from around me. I felt whole again.

I told the volunteer that this was the dog that I wanted and proceeded to made arrangements to pick her up on the following Monday after she had been spayed. Since it was only Friday, I didn't know how I was going to make it through the weekend. Finally, we left her and drove to the PGA Show. All the rest of that day and the next, while I was at the show, I tried to think of the perfect name for my new dog. On Saturday, as was our custom, Dad and I went to one of the parties that are held each year before the Super Bowl kicks off early the next evening. The year before we had gone to the party put on by Head Golf and had enjoyed ourselves, so we decided to do it again. At the last party I had used Muffin's name in the football pool and had won. When I got to this party, I told some people about my new dog and one of them commented that it was like getting a second chance at having a wonderful pet. A light bulb clicked on in my head and I knew immediately that my new dog's name would be "Mulligan." Mulligan is a golf term that refers to a free second tee shot, allowed in many casual games, on the first hole. And since it was a second chance for her, it was a perfect fit for my new dog. Now that I had the name, when it came time to enter the football pool, I naturally wrote down "Mulligan." As luck would have it, she won the $138 pool. To me, it was a very good sign. When the winner's name was announced at the party, a new rule was invoked by Head Golf President Jerry Astry that went into effect the following year: no animals were eligible to participate in the Head Golf Super Bowl Party football pool.

When Monday finally arrived, I was excited about picking up Mulligan at the Humane Society. At the facility, I was told that she was a Westie mix and would probably max out at about 20–25 pounds. When she was brought out, she recognized me at once and proceeded to lick my hands and face. I didn't mention it at the time, but I was sure that the dog I had picked out the previous Friday was gray—the dog I was now holding was white. I let it pass because I was too excited about taking her home to my mother and sister. What I was more concerned about was the fact that Mulligan was not housebroken and we had a four-hour trip ahead of us. It turned out that there was no need to worry. The moment we got into the car, Mulligan fell asleep and didn't wake up until we pulled into our driveway. Mom and Barbara were waiting to see her and fell in love with her at first sight. One of the first things that Barbara said was, "Didn't you tell me she was gray?" When I nodded in agreement, Barbara came up with a theory that made me feel sure that Mulligan was the dog for me. She said that Muffin was mostly white and that when I first saw Mulligan she *was* gray. However, once I chose her, Muffin sent me a signal to let me know she agreed with my choice by changing Mulligan's color from gray to white. The truth, I'm sure, was that Mulligan was just dirty and a nice bath brought out her true color. At least I *think* that explains it.

The next day, Barbara made a big banner that read: The Winner. We hung it up and Dad, Mulligan, and I posed for a photograph. We sent it and an announcement to all of our friends. The announcement read:

> *After an exhausting nationwide talent search, I have adopted another dog. We found her at the Orlando Humane Society. Her name is Mulligan because she is my second dog and because it is a second chance for her.*

Every day with Mulligan was a learning experience. She was a little mischievous, but that was to be expected since she was still a puppy. Not long after I got her, I decided that I was going to try to teach her some things so that she might become a part of my show. I hadn't done that with Muffin so I was entering a whole new arena. As luck would have it, I won six free obedience lessons at the annual Humane Society banquet. When I contacted the trainer, Tracy Tenner, she asked me what I wanted to accomplish with the lessons. I said, "I'd like to teach her to somehow tee up a golf ball. Plus, find out what it takes to become a certified service dog."

Tracy assigned this task to one of her assistants, Yosi Samuels, who was game for the undertaking. It took about a month to teach Mulligan to tee up a ball. It was fun working with her because I could almost see the lightbulb go off in her head when she got the hang of a new trick. She loved to please me and was eager to learn. From teeing up the golf ball we moved on to teaching her how to wave. Finally, we taught her how to make a little bow to use at the end of the show. All of this occurred with Yosi's guidance, but on my own I was trying to teach her how to bark on command. I would signal her with a single finger when I wanted her to bark one time. For example I would say, "When you play golf you want to hit the ball in the fairway, not in the _____. I moved my finger and she would bark once, *"Ruff!"* Another question I asked her was who hit 60 home runs (this was long before McGwire, Sosa, and Bonds). She would then bark two times and it sounded like Babe Ruth (well, sort of). The last thing we came up with was the "tissue trick." I would pretend to sneeze and Mulligan would run over to a nearby tissue box, grab one, and bring it back to me. Adding Mulligan and her tricks to my show gave it a whole new dimension. She was definitely a social butterfly. I would say, "Okay, Mulligan, go work the crowd," and off she would go to visit with the spectators. It was great and I loved working with her.

When I had Muffin, she was basically my personal dog—sticking to me like glue and rarely leaving my side. She seemed to know clearly that her job was to keep up my spirits and comfort me.

Mulligan, on the other hand, seemed to love everyone in the family equally and would spend time visiting them in different rooms of the house. Most nights, Mulligan would sleep in my bed. On occasion, though, my dad would say to her, "Mulligan, what's wrong? You haven't slept in our room for two weeks." Many times after he would say that, Mulligan would wait for me to fall asleep, then jump off my bed and go sleep in my parents' room.

For my mother's 75th birthday, my dad, Barbara, and I decided to take her to a fancy Italian restaurant in a limousine. We knew that we had no chance of sneaking Mulligan into the restaurant but we didn't want to leave her at home, either, so we brought her along in the limo. When we got there, I told Mulligan that she had to stay in the limo with the driver. We assumed, I guess, that the driver would wait in the parking lot and Mulligan would just go to sleep. When we got back into the car after dinner, however, we noticed the distinct smell of cooked hamburger. The driver then told us that he had taken "Miss Mulligan" for a cruise along the Fort Lauderdale beachfront and had capped off the trip with a visit to a McDonald's. Mulligan seemed pretty pleased about the whole evening.

As soon as we felt that Mulligan had learned her tricks pretty well, Yosi and I began to put all of our efforts into preparing Mulligan for her Service Dog test. I wanted her to be able to help me with some simple tasks that would make my everyday life easier. We worked really hard and Mulligan passed the test on the first attempt. By passing, she no longer had to be carried around from place to place in a duffel bag and could wear a cape that said "Working Service Dog." This designation meant that she had free access into hotels, restaurants, airplanes, and all kinds of other places that are normally off-limits to pets.

Wearing her cape, Mulligan was now able to accompany me to Broadway shows, movies, and baseball games. At a Texas Rangers home baseball game once, I signaled to a hot dog vendor that I wanted to buy one. When he came over and saw Mulligan sitting on my lap, he picked her up so that the crowd could see her and shouted, "Here's a real hot dog!"

The great thing about this was that I was no longer hassled about taking my dog with me. Wherever I wanted to go, Mulligan could go too. She gambled with me in Atlantic City and Las Vegas and sat with me during the Siegfried and Roy show in Vegas. One time in Atlantic City, I was winning at the blackjack table and my dealer was enjoying the fact that Mulligan was sitting on my lap. Whenever I wanted a "hit," I would take Mulligan's paw and scratch it across the table to indicate that I wanted another card. When I wanted to "stay," Mulligan waved her paw to signal that she was happy with her cards. When it was time to change dealers, the new person did not seem to be as much of a dog lover as the first dealer. He called over the pit boss and said, "What's the story with this dog? Is it okay for the dog to play?" The pit boss, who had been watching us from the beginning, didn't even blink. "Yeah," he responded, "da dog can play. Da dog's alright."

One year I went to Minneapolis to do my show at the Great Minnesota Golf Show in the Metrodome. While I was there I was invited to appear on the "Late Sunday Night Sports Show," a local TV program hosted by Mark Rosen. Unfortunately, I'd had the flu for a few days and I was not interested in staying up until 10:30 p.m. I declined the offer and suggested that we try to do it the next time I was in Minneapolis.

Mark said, " We'll pay you $750 for your appearance."

Instantly, I replied, "What time is the limo picking me up?"

When I got to the studio and took my seat on the set, I put Mulligan in the chair beside me and she immediately fell asleep. My interview lasted about 15 minutes of the 30-minute show. At a commercial break, Mark thanked me for coming and I started to get up. As usual, Mulligan awakened when she heard me stand and I picked up her leash to leave. Mark stopped me and asked, "Oh, by the way, can the dog stay?"

Naturally, I said sure. So for the rest of the show Mulligan sat in Mark's lap. Every once in a while they would flash a message across the screen indicating that Mulligan was the "co-host." It was pretty funny. Even funnier was what happened at the airport the next day while we were waiting to catch a flight back to Fort Lauderdale. Several people came up to us and said, "Isn't that Mulligan, the dog that was on Mark Rosen's show last night?" When I told them that it was the same dog, they usually smiled or nodded, then, as an afterthought, asked, "You were on the show, too, right?" Upstaged by my own dog.

Mulligan added so much to my life. When I lost Muffin, I did not think that I would ever find a dog that I would love as much as her. Mulligan was the perfect dog to follow Muffin. In many instances, if you believe in it, I think Mulligan could easily have been a reincarnation of Muffin. My long and arduous search only reinforced my feelings that you must always persevere in your pursuit of your dreams and the things that make you happy.

– Chapter 13 –

The Worst Day of My Life

IN OCTOBER OF 1996, we had been on our usual six-month odyssey and our last scheduled show was at the Walt Disney World Golf Classic in Orlando, Florida. I had performed at Disney World countless times and it was there, in fact, where I had made my first major public appearance all those years ago. As they had done in the past, the event's officials had made arrangements for us to park the motor home at "Fort Wilderness" and we were looking forward to a day or two of relaxation at the theme park before the show. The first day, Barbara, Mulligan, and I went to Epcot Center. We had a great time and everywhere we went people stopped to say hi and to pet Mulligan. She was wearing her official Service Dog cape as always, but we had also found a small Mickey Mouse hat that we were able to put on her head. At one point, a group of Japanese tourists stopped us because they all wanted to have their picture taken with Mulligan.

My show was scheduled for the next afternoon. When it was over, our plan was to make the four-hour drive to our home near Fort Lauderdale. I had been on the road since April and I was really looking forward to getting home. I remember it was a bright sunny day and there was a nice crowd for the show. Mulligan performed her opening act duties beautifully and then followed her usual routine of visiting with everyone in the crowd. She was her normal social butterfly self and made sure she didn't miss anyone in the audience. She would go up to all the kids, lick their faces, and sit next to them for a minute while they petted her. She also had a little bit of the devil in her and before you knew it, she would steal your hot dogs or cookies and drink your soda, getting into whatever mischief she could. Once the show started, she found a comfortable spot in the audience and would hang out until the show was over. Everyone loved Mulligan because she was so special.

The last shot in the show is the rapid-fire machine gun shot. I hit five balls in succession as they roll down a ramp onto a board. Just as Barbara rolled the last ball down the ramp, something in the audience must have scared Mulligan because she began to run toward me. I never saw her because I was already into my down-swing and looking at the spot where the next ball would be. Barbara, who was at ground level rolling the balls, got a glimpse of Mulligan but everything happened so quickly that there was nothing that she could do. The horror that unfolded next is still, after all these years, so vivid in her mind:

"I knew Mulligan was behind me sitting in the crowd. I was on one knee rolling the last ball down the ramp and out of the corner of my eye I saw Mulligan run by me. I lunged for her but missed and as Dennis swung his club she was struck in the head. Even today, if I close my eyes, I can see the whole thing so clearly. It's like a movie that replays in my head over and over. Not only can I see it happening in my mind visually, but I can also hear the sound, that dull thud, and even now when I roll the balls down the ramp I still every once in a while get chills."

To this day, we are still not sure what caused Mulligan to run toward me. The moment it happened, Barbara scooped her up and started to give her CPR. Luckily, there was a veterinarian and a registered nurse in the crowd and they helped as best as they could. An EMS vehicle arrived and we put Mulligan inside and took her to a nearby animal hospital. Everything was in chaos and I knew she was seriously hurt. Barbara rode with Mulligan while I was driven over in another car. When I got to the clinic, Barbara was standing next to Mulligan, crying and comforting her. Up to then, Mulligan had not been responsive. But when she heard the tapping of my crutches on the floor, she started to wag her tail. She was dying but when she heard that sound, she knew I was there. *That's* how close our bond was.

For the next three days, Mulligan hung in there and fought valiantly and Barbara and I were with her almost the entire time. I was hoping for a miracle and praying that she would recover. On the third day, though, she had a seizure and just about all hope was gone after that. She had tubes and wires everywhere and it was at this point that I realized I was keeping her alive for me and not for her and I decided that she had suffered enough. I talked to her and mentioned all of the good times we had had together and told her how much I loved her. Then I told the vet that it was time and I held her in my arms while he administered the shot. It was over in seconds and I was thankful that she went peacefully.

The trip back home — that we had eagerly anticipated only days before — was excruciating. Both Barbara and I were totally exhausted from the ordeal. We brought Mulligan home with us and took her to our wonderful local vet, Dr. David Eich, for cremation. We then buried her in my backyard next to Muffin and I know the two of them are safe together.

That experience was the worst thing that ever happened to me — far worse than my own paralyzing accident. I was physically ill over Mulligan's death for a long time. I had terrible chest pains for months and felt like I had a hundred-pound weight on me. Nothing in my life could ever compare to the pain I felt. I had loved that dog so much. Friends and family tried to comfort me but I wouldn't let anyone get close to me. Much later, Barbara told me that when my friend Slugger White called (he's a PGA Tour official and a friend from my college days), she told him, "I don't think Dennis will ever pick up a golf club again." I was totally devastated and beyond being consoled by anyone.

Fortunately, though, time has a way of easing the pain. I did—after what seemed like an eternity—go on. Thankfully, I also picked up my golf clubs again and eventually began to search for another dog. I knew that I wouldn't feel totally alive unless I had another one. A dog can give such unconditional love and put so much joy in your life. At least that's the way it has been for me. A day never goes by without my thinking about my first two loyal pals, Muffin and Mulligan.

Like a lot of people, my mind-set has been shaped by the events in my life. As a result, I have not always been the most optimistic person in the world. Mulligan's tragic death, unfortunately, caused me to frequently expect the worst. Yet, strange as it sounds, I also felt that I could face any new adversity after what had happened. Truthfully, though, no amount of time will ever totally eliminate the pain and memory of that horrible day.

It sounds trite, but life just isn't fair sometimes.

The Little Cowboy—1952, age 3.

The Walters family in 1956 — Dad, Barbara (age 10), Mom, and me (age 7).

New Jersey State Junior, The Knoll Golf Club, June 1967 — age 17.

High school graduation, Neptune High School, June 1967 — age 17.

My sophomore year at North Texas State University, 1968 — age 19.

North Texas State University golf team 1968–1969 — age 18.
Back row (L to R): Bob Henson, Randy Moore, Coach Herb Ferrill, Bernie
Auerett, me (Dennis Walters), Gary Kirwin. Front row (L to R): Rip Collins,
David Stanley, Hale Baugh, Tom Porter, Guy Cullins, Bill Powell.

Hitting practice balls from my wheelchair at Crystal Lago Country Club in 1975, just a little more than a year after the accident.

Practice putting at Crystal Lago Country Club in Pompano Beach, Florida, in 1976.

Playing golf at Covered Bridge Golf Club in Freehold, New Jersey, in 1976 in one of the early golf cart versions.

Dad watching me hit practice balls in 1977.

The Met Golf Writers Dinner in 1978 in New York at the Rye Town Hilton Inn, where I received the Ben Hogan Award. (L to R): then PGA Tour Commissioner Deane Beman, Bob Rosburg, me, Red Hoffman, and Lincoln Werdan.

Dad watching me practice my progression elevated trick shot at one of my shows.

Former President George H.W. Bush and Muffin, Washington, D.C., 1990.

Me, the King (Arnold Palmer), and Muffin at a golf outing in the early 1990s.

The Movie Star—Mulligan—in 1993.

Ben Hogan, me, and Mulligan at Shady Oaks Country Club in Fort Worth, Texas, in the early 1990s.

Gene Sarazen and me at the Sarazen World Open in 1997.

Receiving the Graffis Award in Phoenix in 1994 from the National Golf Foundation. Dad, Mom, me, and Barbara.

Tiger, me, and Benji Hogan at the Tiger Woods Foundation Clinic in Atlanta in 1999.

Actor Chevy Chase, me, and Benji Hogan at the Christopher Reeve Golf Tournament, 2001.

NBA star Michael Jordan, Benji Hogan, and me at the Mario Lemieux
Tournament in Pittsburgh, 2000.

Lord Byron Nelson, Benji Hogan, and me at the Byron Nelson Classic in the
spring of 2000.

Dennis Walters—Swing sequence overview by David Leadbetter of the David Leadbetter Golf Academy

I remember Dennis Walters prior to his accident, when he played on the South African professional circuit. He was an excellent player and a fine ball striker. Obviously, he had to make many adaptations after his debilitating accident, but having seen many of his clinics in recent years, he has lost none of his great hand-eye coordination. He hits the ball very solidly and straight, and has an efficiency of motion that many golfers would benefit tremendously from. What he lacks in mobility he makes up for in consistency and repetitiveness of motion. So much emphasis over the years has been put on the leg action in the swing—obviously, in Dennis's case there is no leg action to speak of. His swing is not just *all* hands and arms, however. His swivel chair allows him to make use of his trunk—albeit in a much more reduced fashion. As with all good swings, consistency is based on synchronizing the trunk movement with that of the hands and arms— Dennis epitomizes this.

Address and Takeaway: The most noticeable feature here, with Dennis hitting a driver, is his upper body 'tilt.' By setting his right shoulder low he has a little more of his body weight on his right side—this will encourage him to catch the ball slightly on the upswing, which is so necessary in hitting solid tee shots.

Top of the swing: This top of the backswing position shows Dennis's flexibility. He has obvious minimal hip rotation, yet a very full shoulder and chest rotation. He is fully coiled at this point. Notice the stretching of the shirt on the left side of his torso. Dennis is in a beautifully compact "top of the backswing" slot—with a very full wrist-cock. This loaded position is very powerful—it gives one the impression of a major league baseball player preparing to hit one out of the park.

Downswing: Dennis is starting to unwind his torso—notice the looseness in the left side of his shirt. The arms are moving down in conjunction with the unwinding of his torso. Note how the right elbow is returning to his right hip and the club is approaching the ball on a shallow "inside" plane—a perfect angle to draw the ball from.

Impact: Dennis epitomizes what many players think about impact—returning to their address position. His head is nicely behind the ball and the left shoulder, left hand and shaft form almost a straight line—a sure sign of a square face at impact. All the energy at this point has been transferred from the torso into the clubhead.

Post Impact: We now see a full release of the right arm and right hand—with the right shoulder working down and through. This is a good image for all golfers to copy with the driver.

Three-quarter Follow-through position: The wrists have now almost totally re-hinged. With the aid of his swivel chair, he has maintained the angle of his spine well into the finish—another key to consistency.

Finish: A full "wraparound" finish indicates good acceleration. If you simply observe Dennis's upper torso, it has all the signs of a classic follow-through. What Dennis lacks in lower body mobility he more than makes up with great balance, stability, and courage.

– Chapter 14 –

Benji Hogan

I KNEW IT WOULDN'T BE EASY to find a new dog. After Mulligan's death, the people from the Disney tournament were fabulous, especially Jim Kern who is now in charge of golf operations for Disney. I was definitely looking for a shaggy *Benji*-type movie dog and I was hoping that maybe Universal had a dog that didn't make it into the film but would make a terrific pet. At the urging of my friend, Wayne Warms, I called Jim to see if he and the Disney folks would call Universal Studios. Sure enough, after a few phone calls, Jim called to say that they had located a dog in South Carolina that was a *Benji* look-alike. He told me that they were sending me a video of the dog and were making arrangements for the dog to be flown to Orlando. My dad and I drove to the airport to meet the plane and the anxiety and excitement was almost more than I could handle.

Since Mulligan's accident had been widely covered by the Golf Channel and the local newspapers, Disney had notified them of the good news and there were reporters at the airport to cover the story. Unfortunately, this story did not have a happy ending. When the dog arrived, she was much larger than they had originally told us. I was looking for a small dog about 20–25 pounds. This dog, while looking like Benji, was so big that there was no way she would ever be able to sit beside me on the golf cart, let alone fit on my lap. The trainer who brought the dog from South Carolina was very nice but she quickly saw my disappointment. She insisted that I take the dog home for a few days with no obligations. With heavy hearts, my dad and I started out for home. The poor dog was just a bundle of nerves and got carsick before we had driven very far. I knew that this was not a good sign because of all the traveling I do during my touring season. When we got to my house, my mom and sister were anxiously waiting to see the dog. Upon seeing her, Barbara decided that we should call her Moose. The dog slept with me that first night and took up half the bed. I tried to comfort her and work on a bonding process but it just didn't take. I even took her to a couple of my shows to see how that would work. But, in the end, I knew that I needed to give her back. She would be a great pet for some other family but she was just not the dog for me. It was time to start looking again.

The first call I made was, once again, to my friend Joanne Roman at the Broward County Humane Society. Joanne gave me a list of 45 animal shelters and pounds that stretched from Miami to Daytona Beach on the east along the west coast of Florida. With the list in hand, Dad and I got in the van and hit the road in an attempt to visit every facility. After each stop (all unsuccessful), I left a written description of the dog I was looking for in hopes that someone would give me a call if they found a suitable dog. The description was simple: female, 20 pounds, looks like "Benji." After 10 disappointing days, we returned home.

Following our trip, I went to the Miami dog pound every day. On one of my visits I happened to stop at the puppy room. Usually I bypassed this area because I wanted a dog that was between one and two years old. When I went in, a staff member was in the process of putting a bedraggled mess of a puppy into one of the cages. The puppy caught my eye because it fit my description to a tee. When I asked about it, I was told that the puppy had recently been found in the city of Hialeah, just outside Miami. The poor thing was full of fleas, had no hair on its tail, and was estimated to be about three months old. However, I knew that those were minor problems that could be taken care of with a little TLC. Its *major* problem, unfortunately, was that it was a male. I called Barbara on my cell phone and asked her for advice.

"You finally found a dog that interests you," she said. "Put your name on the list to reserve him, and we'll talk about it for a few days."

Since it took about six days to formally adopt a dog, I did what Barbara suggested and reserved the little guy. I then visited each day, bringing along family members and friends—even an assistant from our vet's office—to help me decide. After a bath and a good combing, the puppy looked healthier and happier. I also thought it was a good sign that when I came down the hall toward his cage, he would hear me and the cage would begin to shake. I loved his sandy colored hair, too, so I decided that I would call him "Bunker" if I took him. He was always friendly and eager to see me, but unlike my other dogs, he was not all that affectionate.

Since my previous dogs had been females, I incorrectly believed that the puppy's lack of affection was because he was a male. As the sixth day approached, I began to get apprehensive and could tell that I was looking for excuses not to take the dog. Apparently, my sister could see it, too, because she asked me what was wrong. I expressed my apprehension and said that I wasn't sure that I wanted to spend the next 15 years with a dog that wasn't capable of giving me the love and affection that I had been used to.

"Then don't get it," she replied. "Keep looking. You'll find the right one."

I felt as if a big weight had been lifted off my shoulders and called the pound to say that I had changed my mind. Also helping me make the decision was the fact that Bunker was by now the best-looking dog in the facility. I was sure that he would find a good home.

Six more weeks passed without any luck. Then out of the blue one day, Bobbi McGary called me from Pets in Distress and said that she had the perfect dog for me. She said it weighed about 20 pounds and looked like Benji. When she told me that that the dog was a male, I thanked her but said I wasn't interested. She was undeterred.

"If you don't take him," she said, "he's so cute that we will not have any trouble whatsoever placing him with another family. I am bringing him right over," she added.

I was outside in my wheelchair when she pulled into our driveway and parked. When she came around one end of her car, strolling along beside her was a cocky little dog with a bandana around his neck. He saw me sitting there, broke away from the lady and jumped right into my lap and started kissing my face. To my surprise, he looked exactly like the dog I had seen at the Miami pound.

When I looked the dog over, I noticed that he had the exact same birthmark on his back that Bunker had. When I asked the lady where she got him, she told me he had come from the Miami dog pound. Apparently, he had been adopted by a Pets in Distress volunteer after I had turned him down. (Pets in Distress is an organization that goes to different shelters and adopts dogs, cares for them initially, and then places them in good homes.) After the volunteer took the dog home, he noticed that the dog's abdomen was swollen. He took the dog back and was told by the veterinarian on duty that the dog evidently had a tumor and would have to be put to sleep. The volunteer told the vet that the swelling hadn't been there earlier, but the vet wouldn't change his diagnosis and the puppy was seemingly doomed. The Pets in Distress volunteer asked the vet when the procedure would take place and was told it would happen in a few minutes. Thinking quickly, the volunteer picked up the dog when the vet's back was turned and dognapped him. He then drove the puppy to another vet. This vet examined him and said that when the dog had been neutered, the surgery was botched and the swelling was caused by a collection of urine in his abdomen. He reoperated on the dog and corrected the situation. After surgery, the dog recovered in Bobbi McGary's house for about five weeks.

After hearing this story, I decided that it was just meant to be that I keep the dog. Think about it. What are the odds that after six weeks I would have a second opportunity to adopt the same dog? On top of that, this unaffectionate male puppy had turned into a sweet lovable little guy. I decided to keep him and it turned out to be one of the best and happiest decisions of my life. From day one, the little guy was a mixture of laughs and headaches. The first time I took him back to the vet I knew he was destined to be a lady-killer. As I walked into the office, the receptionist said, "Hey, it's Biscuit!" She explained that she had kept him at her house right after his surgery. "When he first came here his name was Cupcake," she told me, "but I didn't like that name so I changed it to Biscuit. He slept with me for a few days."

As I was leaving the vet's office that day, a volunteer from Pets in Distress was about to enter. "Hey, Cookie," she said to the dog, "how are you doing?"

When she saw the surprised look on my face, she told me that she fostered dogs in her home and that when he came to her house his name was Biscuit. "I didn't think that name suited him," she said, "so I changed it to Cookie. He slept at my house for a few days."

Whoever he was, Cupcake-Biscuit-Cookie appeared to have slept with quite a few girls in Broward County. The lucky dog.

Benji Hogan came to live with me just after Christmas of 1996. My hero, Ben Hogan, was pretty ill at the time so I decided to write a letter to Mrs. Hogan to inform them about my new pal and good fortune:

Dear Mrs. Hogan,

I wanted to let you and Mr. Hogan know about my good news. I found a new dog and named him after your husband. I hope this news puts a smile on your faces. Out of love and respect, a lot of people have named their dogs in honor of Mr. Hogan and I certainly want to be included in that group. I know your husband is a real dog lover. In fact, he had his picture taken with one of my other dogs, Muffin. My new dog looks just like the dog in the movie Benji, and to honor Mr. Hogan in this way, I will call him Benji Hogan. I hope our paths cross again soon so that both you and Mr. Hogan can meet him.

Sincerely,

Dennis Walters

I was so thrilled about finally finding another dog that we decided to let all our friends know that the search was over. So Barbara and I made up the following poem:

To all our friends who shared our blues
We want to tell you our good news.
The very creature that you see
Was found by Pets in Distress just for me.
He spent some time at the Miami pound
But now every day will include an 18- hole round.
Since golf is definitely his game
We chose Hogan as his name.

We wanted to send a picture of Benji Hogan along with the poem so I called my friend, Dave Decoteau, at Downtown Photos in Fort Lauderdale and asked him if he would take some photos. I could tell he wasn't too fired up about it because he explained he had recently spent over an hour photographing an uncooperative poodle. But I convinced him, and when we arrived at the studio Dave asked, "Do you think your dog would sit on that stool?"

Well, as luck would have it, in the few days that I'd had Hogan, I had taught him to sit. However, that was as far as I had gotten. Amazingly, Hogan jumped right up on the stool and sat down and posed for pictures like he had been doing it his whole life. Dave shot two rolls of film in 10 minutes and said, "Dennis, that is one smart dog."

"Just don't ask him to do anything else," I replied.

*　*　*

Living with Hogan was not easy at first. He was far from perfect and was constantly getting into mischief. It had been much easier with my other dogs because they were older and were ladies when I got them. The difficult time I was having caused me to turn, once again, to my friend, Tracy Tenner, who had helped me with Mulligan's training. Tracy told me about a world renowned trainer named Phil Hoelcher and said she would call him and see if he could work with Hogan. She contacted him but he said he was too busy. I contacted him myself and pleaded with him until he finally agreed—but only if he could keep the dog with him for at least three weeks. Well, by the time Phil came and got Hogan I was at my wit's end and maybe just a little relieved to see him go. The plan was for Phil to improve Hogan's behavior, and then I would concentrate on teaching him tricks when he returned. Phil said he would keep me apprised of Hogan's progress with daily phone calls. One day he said, "This is the most stubborn dog I have ever seen in my life. I have corrected him more than I have ever corrected the German shepherds that I train."

Phil worked hard with Hogan. One of the things that we had discussed was the great deal of traveling that I do, so he made sure to put Hogan in the front seat of his car a lot in order to get him used to riding in one. On one of those trips, he was taking another dog to an audition for a Kmart commercial so he took Hogan along for the ride. While Phil and the other dog went in for the audition, Hogan stayed in the car with another trainer. Like a scene out of a movie, the producer of the commercial happened to walk by the car, saw Hogan sitting in the front seat, and said, "The search is over. This is just the kind of dog that we're looking for."

Hogan took to "acting" like a duck takes to water. He couldn't wait to go to work and he ended up doing eight commercials for Kmart. I did a show at Harding Park Golf Course in San Francisco once. A boy came up to see Hogan and said, "Hey! That's the Kmart dog I saw on television."

Eventually, Phil began to have some success in turning Hogan's behavior in a positive direction. The bad thing was that it was taking longer than both of us had anticipated. I was anxious to have him home with me, so we decided that after three weeks Hogan would come back so that he and I could start our bonding process. By now it was already well into January and I knew that I had to have Hogan ready to go on the road by May 1. During the two weeks

Hogan was with me, I would work on housebreaking him and teaching him some basic tricks. When it was time for him to return to Phil, the concentration would strictly be on deportment.

I already had a fair amount of dog training skills so I decided to use the same procedures and methods that I had used with Mulligan. I found that by sitting in my wheelchair I was able to work best by placing Hogan on the kitchen table. It was easier for me to have complete control and he was at eye level with me. Repetition works the best and so I set up training sessions every day. I would begin by dividing each trick into steps and repeating each step until Hogan was able to understand it and do it consistently. Early on, I realized that Hogan loved food and enjoyed the learning process. The combination of these two factors made him a perfect candidate to be a performer. While Hogan was a quick study in the area of tricks, he was still not getting the message regarding housebreaking and I was getting very frustrated. Here I had this brilliant dog that had learned to tee up a golf ball and bring me a tissue when I sneezed, and yet he still was not housebroken. At the end of my two-week period, believe me, I was ready to pack him off to Phil's for more behavior lessons. For the next few months we continued following this pattern with great success in the skill areas but little, if any, in the behavior department. At last, though, he finally came around with his behavior and by the time May arrived he was, at long last, housebroken. I could now look forward to taking him on the road with me. By early March, I was anxious to introduce him to his first live audience. Hogan made a brief appearance at the Honda Classic, did a few basic tricks and performed them well. When it was my turn to perform, however, his behavior went downhill. He started crying and barking so I removed him from the show. Luckily, Phil and Tracy were there with me and they took him back to the car. As time went by, we realized that once Hogan began performing he did not like to leave the spotlight. As a consequence, he turned into a real ham.

When I began my tour in May, Barbara went with us. With her along to help me, I was better able to deal with Hogan. Although his behavior was better, he still had a lot to learn. I hoped he would improve as he matured.

In July, two things happened that seemed to make a pivotal difference in Hogan's and my relationship. Barbara was scheduled to fly home and my dad was coming out on the road with me for a month. At about the same time, Phil called and said that Hogan had been hired to do two more commercials. After thinking about it for a while, I decided to send Hogan home with Barbara. I was starting to get very attached to him, but he was still a handful. Another reason for the decision was because it would give Phil a full month to work on Hogan's behavior.

In August, Barbara and Hogan met us in Pittsburgh and my dad went home. I immediately saw a tremendous improvement in Hogan and I think it was partly because he missed me as much as I had missed him. Before he left in July, I had been trying to teach Hogan to bark on command. As I had with Mulligan, I wanted to ask him some simple questions during my show that he could respond to with a bark or two. Such as, "Hogan, where do golfers not want to hit the ball?" Answer: (in the) "Ruff." Phil, however, had felt that there were other more important priorities to deal with so there hadn't been time for me to teach Hogan to bark on cue. Fortunately, though, the commercials that Hogan worked on in July had required that very ability. During the filming, when it was time for Hogan to bark, Phil gave him a signal that he had taught him. It was a high-pitched noise that Phil made with his mouth, but unless you were really listening for it you didn't notice. It worked beautifully.

Luckily, at the beginning of August, I had a break in my schedule for five days and I was able to work with Hogan for several hours each day. I had great success with Hogan following my signal. After about a month, Hogan began to bark the correct amount of times in response to the questions I asked him *without* needing a signal. It was amazing, and I think it was attributable to the incredible bond that we were forming. In the coming months our question and answer sessions got better and better and by Hogan's second year on the road, everyone was trying to figure out how we did this because there was no obvious sign or signal that could be detected. I think that Hogan was so in tune to me — and vice versa — that he must have been picking up some kind of unconscious signal that I was giving him through my body language. As the years have gone by, Hogan and I have continued to refine this process and I can honestly say that in no way do I give him a signal. It's amazing to think that people respond to his feats the way they do. It certainly comes across as his knowing answers to questions that he's asked. He can answer almost any question that he's asked as long as the answer to the question is a number. Even more astounding is the fact that not only will he answer the question that *I* ask him, he'll give the correct answer when asked by *a stranger*. And I honestly do not give him any conscious signal as to what the number of barks should be for a correct answer. What started out as my desire to teach Hogan a simple trick has turned into something beyond my belief and imagination. For my money, Hogan has become one of the strongest opening acts in show business. Which means that I'd better be good, if I'm going to follow him.

At the Crosby golf tournament in Bermuda Run, North Carolina, early in Hogan's career, one of the questions I was asked at the beginning of my show was, "What kind of food are you feeding your dog? He has a beautiful coat." I answered, "It's called Eukanuba, which is a premium brand dog food made by the IAMS Company." A short time later, I received a call from Bryan Brown of IAMS. He said that a representative of his company had been in my audience in North Carolina and was very impressed with Benji Hogan. His company offered to feed him for life. That was fine with me and Benji Hogan was introduced to the world of sponsorship. He wears a Eukanuba bandana, passes out free coupons for his favorite food, and he and I go to a charity golf tournament or two every year representing IAMS to raise funds for animal shelters. Plans have even been made for Benji Hogan to become a founding member of the Eukanuba Elite Team. The Team will travel around the country appearing at trade shows and pet fairs showing people the joys and benefits of pet ownership. Not bad for a dog who had his beginning in the Miami pound. In the May 2002 issue of *Dog Fancy* magazine, you will find a feature story on Benji Hogan.

One thing that I knew would make my life easier was if Hogan, like Mulligan, could pass the test to become a Service Dog. I began Hogan's next phase of training by working toward this goal. As I had hoped, he passed the test with flying colors and as a result he could now accompany me everywhere, from airplanes to restaurants to hotels. Hogan is a pooch that wears many hats: Service Dog, performer, corporate spokesdog and most of all, a loyal companion and friend.

For the last five years Hogan has performed with me all over the country, amazing folks everywhere. He counts among his friends Tiger Woods, Michael Jordan and most of the members of the PGA and Senior PGA Tours. He has even had a chance to sing a duet with the Country & Western singer Vince Gill. As you probably have guessed, the song was, "How Much Is That Doggie in the Window?" Vince sang the song and Hogan barked out the chorus. Other celebrities that have been charmed by Hogan include Celine Dion, Judy Collins, Ray Romano, Joe Pesci, and baseball great Barry Bonds, who actually asked Hogan questions on an airplane.

As bright and smart as Hogan is, he is still capable of getting into mischief. He's a food addict, and at every opportunity he will steal food from someone. At the U.S. Open at Congressional in 1997, Jim Furyk was on the range working hard on his game. When he took a break to grab a sandwich, he also came over to say hello to me. Someone asked to take a picture, so he put his sandwich down on the back of my golf cart for just a second. When he reached back to get it, a few crumbs remained and Hogan was licking his chops. Another victim of Hogan's shenanigans was Tiger's father, Earl. At almost every Tiger Woods Foundation Clinic, Hogan managed to distract Earl long enough to steal his lunch. At the Air Canada Classic, Brandel Chamblee was added to Benji Hogan's hit list when he lost his lunch in the player's dining room. Hogan's reputation precedes him and everyone on Tour knows if you turn your head for a second, you better head on back to the lunch line.

My years with Hogan have been some of the best of my life. When I first got him I had difficulty believing that I could ever find happiness after losing Mulligan. Benji Hogan, like Muffin and Mulligan before him, has filled a tremendous void in my life. I can't ever imagine living my life without the love and joy that these dogs have given me.

– Chapter 15 –

The Real Hogan

AUGUST 14, 1974

Dear Denny,

Just recently I learned of your unfortunate accident and with your permission I would like to offer my thoughts and a word of encouragement.

We know the human body is a great machine and can absorb many shocks. Even though it may seem slow, recovery is possible provided one has faith, hope, will and determination.

From what I heard about you I am sure you possess these qualities. So please keep battling and you will soon overcome this bad interlude in your life.

All good wishes for your future.

Sincerely,

Ben

It was the worst of times. Worse than I ever thought imaginable. My life had been turned completely upside down and I was totally bewildered, angry, and feeling hopeless. Virtually every day there were times when I wished I could have died. Many nights, as I was about to fall asleep, I prayed that I wouldn't wake up. Awakening in the morning, I dreaded having to live through another day of psychological torture and physical futility, and I wished that my family would slip me a pill to end it all.

I did not think that I could ever be more miserable. One particular day, though, for some reason, I was. My depression was so deep that I didn't even want to consider living another day. A nurse took me on a gurney for some tests but I didn't care. I simply did not want to live the way I was now living. When we got back to my room, the nurse smiled and handed me the mail that was on my bed. To me, in the depth of depression, looking at the mail was the last thing on my mind. Within that mail, however, was a ray of hope. It was a letter from Ben Hogan. Believe me when I say that there is no way to adequately describe how much that letter meant to me. I was desperately in need of a mental boost and just the thought that Ben Hogan would take time out of his day to write me a note provided me with a tremendous psychological lift. He was someone who loved golf as much as I did, and someone who years before had suffered serious life-threatening injuries. Ben Hogan had walked in my shoes, so he knew what I was going through.

His recovery from his near-fatal car accident was a long, slow, and painstaking process. He scratched and clawed his way back from adversity to greatness and I knew that he wanted me to take strength from his words. He understood what I was going through because he had been in a similar position. I can't say for sure, but I think that Mr. Hogan might have actually typed the letter because there were no secretary's initials at the end of the letter. To this day, when I think how he took the time to write to me, it still pumps me up.

Shortly after I got the letter, my friend Wayne Warms came to visit me in the hospital. Wayne had always loved to collect golf memorabilia and I considered him an expert in that area. When I showed him Hogan's letter, he was dismayed to see a small water stain at the bottom and lightly chastised me for ruining its pristine condition. When I told him that I had cried after reading the letter and that my tears caused the stain, he said, "A tear stain. Well, now, that's okay, that's cool."

As I mentioned earlier, my first encounter with Ben Hogan took place at the 1967 U.S. Open at Baltusrol Golf Club in Springfield, New Jersey. I was caddying at the event and every day, as soon as I finished my round, I went to the driving range to watch those great golfers go through their practice routine. On three of those occasions, I was lucky enough to catch Mr. Hogan practicing. Since I had my caddie uniform on, I was able to get inside the ropes and managed to secure a spot right behind the player that many people still consider to be the greatest ball striker of all time. I was not, however, the only one inside the ropes who was observing Mr. Hogan. Several of the other professionals stopped hitting balls and just watched as Mr. Hogan hit pure shot after pure shot. It was a remarkable demonstration of his shot-making abilities and I don't recall many times where other pros simply stopped to watch one of their own. He was simply that good.

Baltusrol has two golf courses, the Upper and Lower. During the tournament, the first hole on the Upper Course was used for the practice range. There was a huge tree on the right side of the fairway. Several of the larger branches of the tree formed a V. In those days, the players had their caddies stand down range and shag balls. Mr. Hogan had his caddie stand on a line so that the V of the branches surrounded the caddie like a picture frame. Mr. Hogan started off with his short irons and shot after shot remained within the V. Almost every shot was hit on a similar trajectory, with the only change being the distance they were hit with his different clubs. Almost everybody who has watched Mr. Hogan hit balls will say that he hits every shot perfectly. I probably watched him for a total of three hours that week and I can tell you that I saw a display of shotmaking second to none. Mr. Hogan did prove he was human because I saw him miss a few. His misses, though, were not by much.

The next time I saw him was for a brief time when I was still in college. Two of my teammates and I (Guy Cullins and Wayne Wright), along with Eddie Vossler from Texas Christian University, were playing a friendly round at Shady Oaks Country Club in

Fort Worth, Texas, the club that Mr. Hogan called home. We were having a great day. On the par-3 16th hole, all four of us hit our tee shots to within eight feet of the flagstick. As we headed for the green we unexpectedly met up with Mr. Hogan, who was out walking the course for exercise. He also had his putter and three balls with him so that he could get in a little putting practice. Eddie had shagged balls for Mr. Hogan so he said hello and introduced us. Imagine us college kids getting to shake hands with Mr. Hogan! The five of us continued on to the green and when we got there, Mr. Hogan said, "Nice shots, boys. Keep up the good work." He then said goodbye and continued on his walk. This snapshot in time put us all in a state of awe and not a single one of us came close to making our little birdie putt because we were still thinking about our short walk with one of golf's greatest legends.

The next time I saw Mr. Hogan was in 1970, the last time he played in the Colonial National Invitational at Colonial Country Club in Fort Worth. I took two days off from school and followed him for 36 holes, often getting very close to him for many of his shots. When it began to rain during the last nine holes, the gallery dwindled and I had no trouble getting good views of his play. It seemed as if he had the correct shot for every hole. If the hole went left to right, that is exactly what Mr. Hogan's tee shot did. If the hole went right to left, so did Mr. Hogan's shot. He played precision golf, and even though he did not score well that day, he was clearly a master of the game.

Up to this point, I had only spent a few minutes talking to Mr. Hogan. In the late '70s, when I was in the early stages of the Dennis Walters Golf Show, I was asked to be part of the clinic that would be held during the Colonial National Invitational. Lee Trevino and I did the clinic together and afterward I was invited to a dinner at the club. I got to the dinner early that evening and was the only one in the room. I was looking around at all the pictures and heard someone else come in. When I saw that it was Ben Hogan, I mustered up some courage and hiked over to him on my crutches to introduce myself. I said, "Hi, Mr. Hogan. My name is

Dennis Walters and it's nice to see you." He replied, "I know who you are." I thanked him for writing me the letter after my accident and told him how much it had meant to me. I even told him about the depressed mood that I had been in prior to receiving it. I shared with him the story of the tear stain and let him know how much he really brightened up an otherwise awful time in my life.

I then asked him if he had been at the clinic to see my show. He said he wasn't because he didn't want to cause a distraction while Lee and I were conducting the clinic. He assured me, though, that a Hogan Company executive had been there and had given him a detailed report of how it went. Mr. Hogan congratulated me on a great show. Just then a waiter came in to see if we wanted anything to drink. Mr. Hogan ordered a glass of white wine. I was not much of a drinker but I said, "I'll have the same." To me, being in the same room with Mr. Hogan was way beyond cool. I asked my hero how he was playing and he said it was hard for him because of all his aches and pains. I could tell that it really bothered him. I said, "If they let us use a cart, maybe we can both play in this tournament." He laughed and I really got the feeling that he appreciated my sense of humor.

Some years later we were asked to do a show at Shady Oaks Country Club. I called Mike Wright, the head professional, and asked him if he could arrange for me to meet with Mr. Hogan. When my dad and I got to the club, we set up a golf cart with my portable seat and headed over to the driving range. Passing the clubhouse, we saw Mr. Hogan at his usual table in the grill. We parked the cart and were about to go inside but he came out to greet us. I introduced him to my dad and my dog, Muffin. Mr. Hogan loved dogs and Muffin licked his hand as he was petting her. He asked me how I was hitting the ball and wanted to know if my swing felt good. He was aware that I was doing my show the next day so I told him I really wanted him to stop by and see me hit the ball. After talking another few minutes, I asked Mr. Hogan if he would mind taking a picture with Muffin and me. My dad, who had a history of taking photos that cut off people's heads, was very nervous about taking this shot. I told him, "Whatever you do, don't choke when you take this picture." (I'm happy to report that he didn't.)

Mr. Hogan didn't seem in a hurry to leave us, so I took advantage of this good fortune and asked him if he would sign my copy of his book *Power Golf.* I asked him to inscribe it to Dennis and Muffin. When he finished writing, I decided to really push my luck and ask him to sign a golf ball and my golf hat. I was overjoyed when he agreed. After Mr. Hogan left, I opened my *Power Golf* book and saw that the inscription said "To Dennis and Fuffin." I was disappointed but Wayne told me later that it was the kind of error that everyone who collects baseball cards looks for. The mistake made it more valuable, Wayne said, and it helped me to realize what a treasure I had.

My memory of Mr. Hogan that day was that he was nice, humble, and genuine—just the opposite of the cold, aloof man the media often described. He may have been that way at times, but I was fortunate to see a different side of this wonderful man and, believe me, he was a warm and caring individual. I saw Mr. Hogan later in the day and told him that I wished he had seen me hit some shots. To my surprise he said, "I was watching you from the clubhouse and you were swinging well." Then he said, "You might be the best golfer [of all of us]." He was looking me right in the eye and I immediately understood what he was saying. It was a huge compliment. Having overcome the obstacles and pain that he had encountered, he could well understand what I had been through.

Right about then, to my amazement, he got down in his stance and began showing me how he swung a club. He was in his late 70s at the time and it was very clear how much he still loved the game. When I asked him if he was still able to practice much, I noticed a tear in his eye as he told me it was impossible because of his knee and shoulder injuries. As he was leaving, he took his right index finger and put it across his left one and said, "I hope our paths cross again soon."

Obviously, it was an absolutely awesome day for me. Maybe it was one of the best I've ever had.

*   *   *

I was on my way to do a show in Dallas in the early 1990s and was hoping that I would get a chance to see Mr. Hogan again. I had already called Mike Wright at Shady Oaks and made the request. In the past, I'd always come to Texas by airplane. This time, my dad and I were driving from Florida and I was able to bring my Ben Hogan Award with me. The Golf Writers Association of America had honored me with the award in 1977. It is given annually to the golfer they feel has made the greatest comeback from an injury or illness, and among the past winners were President Dwight Eisenhower, Babe Didrickson-Zaharias, Lee Trevino, and Ken Venturi. I was just starting my career as a performer so this was a tremendous honor for me. At the awards dinner I received my trophy along with a telegram of congratulations from Mr. Hogan. Today that telegram hangs on my hallway wall right next to the tear-stained letter.

Since receiving the trophy, I had desperately wanted to get a photograph of Mr. Hogan and me with the trophy. As soon as I got to Dallas, I called Mike Wright again and was told that a meeting was set up for that very afternoon. I arrived at the club just about the same time that Mr. Hogan and his wife Valerie got there. We exchanged greetings and I thanked him for agreeing to have the photo taken. For the picture, I sat on the right side of my golf cart and Mulligan sat on the driver's side. Just before my dad took the picture, I pointed to Mulligan and said, "We have a rule in our house, Mr. Hogan. If there's ever a fire or a hurricane, the procedure is to get the dog and this trophy, and *then* run."

After my dad took the photo, I asked Mrs. Hogan to get in the picture with us. She said, "No, this is Ben's moment." Later, looking at the trophy she said, "This is really nice. Where did you get it?" Playfully, Mr. Hogan replied and gently poked her in the ribs, "That's the Ben Hogan Award, Silly."

Feeling brave again, I asked him if he would sign the hat I was wearing. "Don't move," he said quickly, "don't even take the hat off your head." After he signed it, he put his thumb up in the air like an artist admiring his latest painting. Mrs. Hogan said, "Why Ben, that's some of your best work." Not long after that we said good-bye and I never saw my hero again.

I had been a fan of his since I was a small boy and just getting interested in golf. I devoured golf magazines and was always on the lookout for articles about the great Ben Hogan. Later, after I went to work at Hollywood Golf Club, Lou Barbaro told me several wonderful stories about him (at one time, Lou and Ben were assistant pros in the Westchester area). I think I always felt drawn to Hogan because we were both slight of build and loved to practice. Even as a boy I admired his work ethic and dedication to the game. As I grew older, this admiration only increased.

I was very lucky to have had the chance to meet with the great man on so many occasions. I think of him often, and when I do it is as if a movie starts in my head and I can recall all the times I was in his presence. When I was struggling and searching for a way that I could continue to play the game I loved, he was my inspiration and a shining example for me to follow. He always said that the answers were "in the dirt" of the practice range and that's exactly where I found them. Ben Hogan was someone who meant a great deal not only to me but also to golfers everywhere. Even today, he is sorely missed, but his spirit and example will live forever.

– Chapter 16 –

Tiger Woods

TIGER WOODS TURNED PROFESSIONAL in September 1996 after winning his unprecedented third consecutive U.S. Amateur Championship. I had been following his amateur career with great interest and was hoping that he would find the same success on the PGA Tour. In the spring of 1997 I was fortunate and proud to be asked to participate in the clinics conducted by the newly-founded Tiger Woods Foundation. From the beginning, I referred to myself as Tiger's "Opening Act," but the relationship between us has been forged by something much more important. We share a mutual love for golf and a desire to help youngsters identify and achieve their dreams.

The clinics are aimed primarily at inner city, underprivileged boys and girls. The excitement that is generated by these clinics is unbelievable. Most of the attendees at these events know about discrimination in one form or another. For me, being in a wheelchair has taught me what discrimination is and has also exposed me to the ugly face of narrow-minded people. For years I hated being seen outside my house in my wheelchair and made it a point to only go places where I could get there comfortably on my crutches. I believe people with disabilities suffer a similar fate to those who are ostracized because of race, religion, or class. Society tends to treat people in wheelchairs as if they have contagious diseases and often people have a difficult time interacting with individuals who have disabilities because they are afraid of catching that dreaded disease: *wheelchairitis.*

When I talk to young people at my shows, I talk from my heart. I tell them that while my problems have been physical, the problems *they* have may be a result of culture and environment. I emphasize that no matter what the problem, they cannot let it keep them from reaching for their dreams. I explain to them that they have to find a way to go over or around or through these obstacles and that with hard work and perseverance, they will find that they can accomplish a lot. My audiences can tell that I had to struggle and claw my way back one step at a time. So I feel that in some small way, the inspiration and the desire that I pass on to them can make a difference. And that makes me feel good.

I look forward to these clinics very much. It's partly because I know how much good is derived from them, and partly because it gives me the opportunity to spend some time with Tiger. Inspiration and encouragement are the themes of these clinics and I like to think that I contribute on both counts. However, all-work-and-no-play is not Tiger's mantra, nor is it mine. A clinic that we put on in Cincinnati, Ohio, one time stands out as truly memorable in the fun department. The star of this particular "show" was not young Mr. Woods, but none other than Benji Hogan. As is usually the case, everyone involved with running the clinic was staying at the same hotel. One night, after having spent a good part of the day working to get the golf course ready for the clinic, we returned to the hotel exhausted. Before saying goodnight, we were all standing in the hallway outside our rooms. While we were talking, someone suggested that the wide hallway would be a perfect place to conduct our version of the Olympic 100-meter dash. Everyone agreed that it was a great idea. All we needed were a few contestants.

American Golf Corporation, the conglomerate that owns and manages golf courses around the U.S., lends a hand with the organization of Tiger's clinics. An intern with the company, Tee Gee Maye, was working a clinic for the first time so we decided that

she had to be initiated into the club. The initiation that we pro-
posed was for her to challenge Benji Hogan—the fastest dog in the
West (well, at least in the hotel)—to a race. My sister Barbara,
Hogan, and Tee Gee walked to one end of the corridor. At the other
end was John Flaschner of American Golf, holding up a white towel.
When John dropped the towel, Barbara let go of Hogan and he
and Tee Gee took off. Hogan flew down the hall and beat her by a
good 10 yards. Following the race, amid gales of laughter, more
challengers took up the gauntlet. Twenty minutes later Hogan was
still undefeated. As my little pal flew down the hall once again,
destroying his latest foe, the elevator doors opened and out walked
Tiger. "What's going on?" he asked with a smile. When he was told
that Hogan was a sure bet for the Gold Medal in the 100, Tiger—
always the competitor—got this gleam in his eye and said, "He
hasn't raced me yet."

So . . . Tiger, Barbara, and Hogan went to the end of the hallway. Tiger had been out to dinner and still had on a sport coat and
a pair of slick-soled leather dress shoes. On the signal, Hogan got
another perfect start but Tiger slipped coming out of the blocks.
It was over before it had hardly started. Sheepishly, Tiger asked for
a rematch and called for Hogan to come back to the starting point.
This time Tiger took off his coat and shoes, determined to win.
They were off on the signal and Tiger ran as fast as he could. Running alongside Tiger, Hogan looked up at him as if to say, "Not bad,
Tiger. You're my stiffest competition so far."

Hogan's margin of victory was about one foot. At the start of
the race, luckily for Tiger, someone had opened the door to his
room, which was at the finish line. Tiger ran through the open door
and leaped onto his bed. He came back out into the hall laughing
and said to Hogan, "Next time we race, I get to wear my spikes."

We had a blast that night.

*   *   *

Benji Hogan loves golf trivia and golf statistics. He especially
enjoys keeping track of Tiger's victories—particularly the majors.

You think I'm kidding, don't you? Well, in May of 2000, at a Tiger Woods Foundation Clinic in Denver, I said to Tiger, "Ask Benji a question." Tiger thought about it for a moment, then said, "How many U.S. Opens have I won?" Hogan just stared at him without barking. Tiger smiled.

A month later, at Pebble Beach, Tiger won his first U.S. Open. Later that summer I said to Tiger, "Remember that question you asked Hogan in Denver? Ask him again." This time when Tiger asked Hogan how many U.S. Opens he had won, Hogan barked a single time. Tiger just smiled that fabulous smile of his and then bent down so Hogan could give him a kiss.

At another clinic later that year after Tiger had won both the U.S. Open *and* the British Open, we greeted each other in our usual way. After we gave each other a high five, I said mischievously, "Been doing anything special lately?"

"Nothing much," Tiger said, grinning. "Just won a couple of tournaments."

I had known that I was going to feel really proud about being part of the Tiger Woods Foundation clinics right from the very first one at Disney World in the spring of 1997. My friend Jim Kern was in charge of golf operations for Disney and he had called to tell me about the clinic that Tiger was going to conduct. He then asked if I would like to participate. As you can imagine, I couldn't get the word "yes" out of my mouth fast enough. They do everything absolutely right at Disney and that clinic was no exception. At one point in the show, someone from Disney asked Tiger, "What happens when you really want to hit the ball a long way? What do you do to make that happen?"

"Well," Tiger replied, "I just use a little wider stance, take a bigger backswing, and swing as hard as I can while still maintaining my balance."

"Think you could demonstrate that for us?" the man asked.

Tiger wound up and let it rip. Without Tiger's knowledge, the Disney people had set up various special effects and as the ball rose into the sky, they set off a fireworks display that resembled the launching of a space shuttle. As the ball dropped to the ground, a loud explosion could be heard. I said to Tiger, "It's going to be pretty hard to top this in any other city."

I look forward to those clinics every year. They're a lot of fun, plus I know that my message is very compatible with the goals of the Tiger Woods Foundation. Those involved are not necessarily trying to make great golfers out of the kids that attend, but they are trying to help them become great *people.* They want the kids to have fun and learn about golf and to learn the valuable life lessons the game teaches us. They also emphasize that the kids need to respect their parents and continue their learning process through education. Another important aspect of these clinics is that once they are over, the Foundation has what they call a "leave behind" program that allows the kids to come back and play golf. It is not a one-time deal, which would be terribly unfair to the kids.

During the 24 clinics that we have done so far, I have come to know Tiger and have been fortunate to have had many opportunities to spend time with him and get to know him a little bit. I have watched him hit a lot of shots and have seen him change from a young PGA rookie into a mature professional golfer. I couldn't be prouder to be the "opening act" for my friend Tiger Woods. Golf is a wonderful game and because of these clinics, people of all backgrounds now have a chance to start playing golf. I look around at the people sitting in the huge bleachers waiting for these clinics to start and I think to my self, *Wow!*

– Chapter 17 –

Arnold Palmer

MY FIRST DOG, Muffin, had her own photo album and it was filled with photos that were taken all over the country. Every time we met a famous person, I would ask him or her to pose for a picture holding Muffin. Little Muffin's album would make anyone jealous. Besides former President George Bush, she was lucky enough to have her photo taken with such notables as Ben Hogan, Sam Snead, Arnold Palmer, Jack Nicklaus, Miss America, and many others. Muffin had obviously been a real star.

When Muffin passed away and I got Mulligan, I decided to carry on the tradition and started an album for her as well. The first person I approached for a photo with Mulligan, who was still a puppy at the time, was Arnold Palmer. It was at a Senior PGA Tour event in Birmingham, Alabama, the Bruno Memorial Classic, and I just took the direct approach and asked Arnie if he would oblige. "Sure," he said. "I'll be happy to." I held up Mulligan and said, "This is the King and I want you to give me your best doggie smile." Arnie patted her on the head saying, "What a nice dog, Dennis. You really know how to pick them." He then took her, as I got ready to take the picture. Just as I was about to snap it, Arnie's thumb somehow ended up in Mulligan's mouth. It wasn't actually a bite, just a puppy nibble. However it did get Arnie's attention. When I had the roll of film developed, the picture clearly showed the King's thumb in Mulligan's mouth. I had the photo enlarged and sent it to him. After enlarging the photo, I realized that another friend of mine, Joe Gibbs, was in the background.

Several months later, I ran into Joe at the U.S. Open at Congressional Country Club in Maryland. Joe had cofounded the Golf Channel with Arnold. I told him that I was going to send him a picture that I thought would give him a chuckle. After he got the photo he called me and said, "I remember that day like it was yesterday—the day your dog bit Arnold Palmer." Apparently Arnold remembered it, too, because several years later, at Mission Inn Golf Club in Howey-in-The-Hills, Florida, I was at a Golf Channel-sponsored event and was just walking into the hotel lobby when Arnie pulled up in his car. He looked at me and said hello, and then looked at Mulligan and, with a big smile on his face, asked, "Is that dog going to bite me again?"

At the Ameritech Senior PGA Tour stop in Chicago one year, I was conducting my show on the left side of the driving range. As usual, my final shot of the show was the rapid-fire machine gun shot. I hit five balls in succession as they roll down a ramp onto a board. Just as I was about to hit the last ball, Arnold walked in from the right side pretty close to the line of fire. He did not see me because the gallery hid me and I couldn't see him for the same reason. The last ball I hit was a smoke ball and, lucky for me, I hit it as planned and the blue smoke exploded way beyond Arnold. That's when I finally saw him and I announced to the crowd, "Hey, it's Arnold Palmer. Let's welcome the King to my show." The crowd gave me one of the biggest roars of my career. Actually, they were cheering for Arnie, but I went along for the ride. Some people probably thought we had this all planned out. Arnie tipped his hat and played right along. He always did seem to have perfect timing.

Arnold Palmer has always been one of my heroes and over the years he has been very nice to me. Several years ago he was kind enough to do the introduction on my promotional video. In the early years of my show, 1978 to be exact, I got an invitation to appear at the Ottawa Hunt Club in Canada and be on the same program as Arnold. What a thrill that was. They had signs up all over the place that said, "Welcome Arnold Palmer" and "Welcome Dennis Walters." There were at least 10,000 people at the clinic and I was scheduled to go on first. Sitting on his bag resting not 10 yards away watching me, was none other the King himself. Boy, oh boy, was I ever nervous. However, the experience was what I needed to be convinced that I could do that type of public performance. It made it crystal clear that I was perfectly capable of pursuing my new dream of becoming a golf entertainer.

– Chapter 18 –

Home on the Range

I REALLY ENJOY DOING CLINICS and exhibitions with the best golfers in the world. I clearly remember a fun show that I did with Fuzzy Zoeller at the 1998 Canon Greater Hartford Open. Fuzzy is a former winner of both the Masters and U.S. Open and is one of a handful of golfers to hold two major titles. After our clinic was over, I asked him to sign a golf ball for me and he kindly agreed. Whenever it's possible, I try to get signed golf balls for my friend Wayne. He has a large collection of golf memorabilia and I attempt to add to it whenever I can. After Fuzzy signed a ball, I placed it in the cup holder on my golf cart. We said goodbye and went our separate ways.

In a show setting like that, I often start talking to people or watch a pro practice and I eventually lose track of time. On that particular occasion, I also did not watch Mulligan as close as I should have. When it was time to leave the range, I noticed that my mischievous little dog had taken the signed ball out of the cup holder and had chewed off about 90% of the cover. About all that was left of Fuzzy's signature were the first three letters. Since I had just finished a phone call to Wayne telling him about the signed ball, I thought, *I am in big trouble.* I thanked Mulligan for putting me in the doghouse with Wayne, and then slipped the chewed-up golf ball in the pocket of my windbreaker.

At dinner that night, my dad and I saw that Fuzzy was eating at the same restaurant so I stopped to say hello. Suddenly remembering the ruined golf ball in my pocket, I asked him if he would mind signing another one for me.

"What are you doing, Dennis," Fuzzy quipped, "selling these things?"

"No," I replied without blinking an eye, "my dog ate the first one."

"Come on," Fuzzy said with a smirk. "Surely you can come up with a better excuse than that."

"The proof is in the pudding, Fuzzy," I said, "and here is the proof." With that I pulled out the chewed-up golf ball and handed it to him. We all had a good laugh, and then Fuzzy came through and signed another golf ball for me.

When I finally saw Wayne, I decided to tease him a bit. I handed him the chewed-up ball first and told him that Mulligan had eaten it. He was clearly disappointed so I let him wallow in it for a minute or two before I handed him the second ball. It has a place of honor in his golf ball collection.

At the LeJet Classic in Abilene, Texas, one year, I was warming up on the range in preparation of doing my show. It was scheduled for later in the day and I was worried about the wind. A ferocious Texas wind was blowing from left to right and I knew that if it continued I would have to make some adjustments. Proceeding with my practice session, I got ready to work on my fire shot. When I do this shot, my dad covers a teed golf ball with a piece of newspaper, pours some lighter fluid on the paper, lights it, and then I hit the ball. Most of the time, the force of air generated by my swing and the impact of the club head will put the fire out. As I prepared to hit one during practice on the range, my dad apparently put a little too much lighter fluid on the paper, because when I hit the ball, the fire did not go out. Instead, the burning paper was carried down the range by the wind. My dad ran after it, but before he could catch it and put it out, it landed right in front of tour pro Tom Weiskopf. Anybody who knows anything about the game knows that Tom has been one of the most talented but most *volatile* players in the history of golf. Naturally, because his concentration and practice session had been disrupted, his first reaction was to get mad. When he saw my dad run over and stomp out the fire, however, he realized who had sent the flaming paper his way. He quickly got over it and we laughed about it for a long time. Just imagine Tom Weiskopf, the volcanic former British Open champion, admonishing *me* for playing with fire.

Since many PGA Tour players are dog lovers, Benji Hogan is always a welcome sight when he shows up on the range. One of his biggest admirers is Stuart Appleby of Australia. Every time Stuart sees Hogan he comes over to pet him and get some dog kisses. One of Stuart's favorite things to do with Hogan is to chip a golf ball over to him because he knows that my dog will immediately start to chew on the cover. Stuart will hit a few more practice shots, then whistle for Hogan to bring over the chewed-up ball. Stuart gets a big kick out of hitting those chewed-up golf balls and watching them fly erratically down the range.

Just before Christmas one year I decided to give Hogan three golf balls to chew on. After he had sufficiently gnawed them, I put them back in their sleeve, wrapped them up, and sent them to Stuart as a present. The next time we saw Stuart, he gave Hogan a big hug and told me how much he enjoyed his gift. Gestures like that make for lasting friendships. Hogan and I could not have a nicer friend than Stuart Appleby.

I was asked to perform at the American Junior Golf Association Rolex Tournament at Disney World in Orlando one year. Also scheduled to put on a show was legendary Canadian ball-striker Moe Norman. After I did my routine I decided to stick around and watch Moe perform his magic. There were a number of good, young golfers in the audience and the head professional brought a big basket of balls for Moe to hit. People who have watched Moe know that he will not quit hitting balls until there aren't any left in the basket. He went through every club in his bag that day, talking nonstop, as he hit ball after ball after ball.

While he was hitting his driver, one of the kids said, "Mr. Norman, you've been hitting the ball really straight. Is that the way you always hit it or are you just having a good day?"

Typical of the unusual way he talks, Moe replied, "Straight, straight, you've got to hit it straight." He then continued hitting ball after ball and would have been there all day if someone hadn't stopped him.

I had hit the ball especially well that day and was feeling pretty good about my swing. After the clinic was all over, a boy came up to me and said, "Moe hit the ball almost as good as you did." Wow, did *that* ever make my day!

* * *

Whenever I perform at a PGA Tour event, I often try to incorporate one or two of the players who are on the range into my show. When I do my left-handed shot, for example, if Mike Weir is practicing I'll ask him if he thinks I can hit it even though I am right-handed. Another one of my favorite lefties is Phil Mickelson. Interacting with these world-class players always seems to make the audience feel more a part of the clinic.

Another tour player who often gets involved with my show is Brad Faxon. Early on he became fascinated with how I performed my triple-hinge shot. The club I use has three universal joints and it bends at all these crazy angles (as you can see in the picture on the cover of this book). The first time Brad tried to hit a ball using this club was during a performance at the Buick Invitational in San Diego. Normally, I'm reluctant to let anyone hit my clubs, but Brad *really* wanted to give it a try. So, with great trepidation, I handed the club to him. It's definitely not an easy club to hit, but once you get the rhythm of the swing it isn't impossible. Rarely, however, can anyone do it the first time and Brad was no exception. He took a big swing and the result was a giant divot that knocked the ball off the tee. Brad wanted to try again, but I said, "Come on, Brad, this is *my* show. Better luck next time."

At the Honda Classic later that year, Brad wandered over to watch my show just as I was about to hit the triple-hinged club. I saw him standing there, introduced him to the crowd, and asked if he wanted to give it another try. He did and the result was the same: zero direct contact with the ball.

That July, I did a clinic at Yale University Golf Club for the Special Olympics. Brad was there too, and, naturally, chomping at the bit to get his hands on my triple-hinged club. He tried it again, and again failed miserably to produce a successful shot. The next day, he and Billy Andrade were sponsoring a charity golf outing in their native state of Rhode Island. They asked me to come and do a clinic and I was pleased to oblige. When I got there, I learned that ESPN was filming the event to be broadcast on its "Inside the PGA Tour" program at a later date. My show began well and they were getting a lot of good footage. When it came time to do the triple hinge, I asked Brad if he wanted to give it another try. He jumped at the chance, no doubt wanting to make a good impression for the hometown crowd. "Okay," I said, "but let me hit one first and show you how to do it." I wound up and absolutely killed it, right down the center of the fairway. I then turned to Brad and said; "Now it's *your* turn." Amid some laughter and shouts of encouragement from the crowd, Brad took an aggressive swing . . . and proceeded to hit it off the toe of the club. The ball went sideways and hit a photographer's camera lens. Fortunately, the photographer was unhurt, everyone had a good laugh, and Brad had finally hit a ball with the triple hinge. Best of all was the fact that the entire episode was caught on film.

Brad has not asked to hit the triple hinge since.

* * *

I saw "Long" John Daly for the first time when I was doing a show in Fort Wayne, Indiana, for the Hogan Tour (later to become the Nike and then the Buy.com Tour). At the very end of the range were large trees that I estimated were about 50 feet tall. To my amazement, I watched as John consistently drove golf balls over the trees. All the other players, even though they could hit the ball well, were lucky if their shots rolled to the *base* of the trees. I was immediately impressed with John's ability and, after meeting him, I instantly liked him, too. A few years later, John and I did a show together at the Atlanta Classic. We were a good team and the crowd was quite enthusiastic. At one point, John walked over to my big bag of tricks and took out my putter. He then teed up a ball, using my putter, sent the ball flying about 280 yards down the middle. To the crowd's delight, John said he was going to put my putter in his bag and use it as a driver.

"Sorry, John," I said, "I can't let you do that. It's my favorite putter."

*   *   *

At the Las Vegas Invitational one year, Hogan and I ran into Fuzzy Zoeller near the locker room and visited with him for a few minutes. I said, "Fuzzy, would you believe it that my dog knows how many majors you've won?"

"C'mon, Dennis," Fuzzy replied, kind of rolling his eyes.

"Ask him," I said.

So Fuzzy did, and Hogan barked twice.

Fuzzy said, "Don't move. Stay right here, I'll be right back."

A few minutes later, Fuzzy returned with his wife and kids. He then asked Hogan how many majors he'd won. Again, Hogan barked twice. The family, especially the children, was quite impressed. They also wanted to know how I was signaling my dog. I denied it, of course.

I'm telling you: Hogan really knows his golf trivia, especially how many majors a player has won. Everyone is aware that Ben Crenshaw knows a lot about golf history. Well, Hogan never fails to amaze Ben with his knowledge. Ben has asked him the most obscure golf trivia questions and Hogan has gotten them right every time. Many times he will walk away from us only to come back a few minutes later because he has thought of another question. I love it when this happens. It also pumps me up knowing how much everyone loves my dog.

At the PGA Tour event in Vancouver, British Columbia once, Benji and I spent a good amount of time on the range with the late Payne Stewart. He and I both liked to fish so we talked about that for a bit. Payne then started asking Hogan questions. He told me he was amazed at Hogan's knowledge, and was sure that I had had a computer chip surgically implanted in Hogan's brain.

Hey, I know what you're thinking. *Yeah, right, Dennis. Your dog knows all these things without being signaled by you. Sure.*

Okay, one last story about how smart Hogan is.

For the last several years, I have been fortunate to participate in the "Jimmy V Celebrity Golf Classic," held in Cary, North Carolina, honoring the late great basketball coach Jimmy Valvano. Michael Jordan played in the event one year. When he arrived on the first tee I announced to the crowd that Benji Hogan knew the number on Michael's jersey. Not having met Hogan and me before, Michael was, of course, skeptical. That changed when Hogan proceeded to bark out the first number (two barks), followed by the second number (three barks), which—as almost everyone on the planet knew—was Jordan's number: 23. Michael absolutely loved it. He then asked Hogan how many NBA championship rings he had won. Hogan barked six times. With that, Michael clapped his hands in glee and pointed to former NBA star Charles Barkley who was standing nearby. "How many rings does *he* have?" Jordan asked Hogan. To Barkley's dismay, Hogan didn't bark even once, which was the correct answer because the teams that Charles had played on had never won an NBA title. The crowd—and Jordan—loved it.

After Michael teed off, Hogan and I followed him for a few holes. On a short par 3, Michael pulled a 7-iron out of his bag, teed up his ball and was about to hit it. Suddenly, he turned to Hogan and asked, "What club should I use?"

Hogan barked six times.

Michael put the 7-iron back in his bag, took out his 6-iron and proceeded to hit his tee shot eight feet from the flagstick. The crowd went wild and it was high-five time for Hogan and Michael Jordan.

True story.

* * *

I have been fortunate to meet the most wonderful professionals when I have performed at PGA Tour events. There are rare exceptions in all cases, of course, but I have been lucky in that I have run into only a few pros that didn't view me as an equal.

It was always my dream to play on the PGA Tour. Even though it didn't turn out that way, I'm proud and happy that I hung in there and created my *own* professional tour.

– Chapter 19 –

Baseball and Golf

YOGI BERRA, the legendary Hall of Fame catcher for the New York Yankees, is well known not only for his baseball skills but also for taking liberties with the English language. One example of these "Yogi-isms" is "It looks like déjà vu all over again." Well, I'm proud to tell you that I was actually in his presence when he came up with my very own "Yogi-ism." Here's how it happened.

I once did a show that preceded a tournament in which Yogi was a participant. After I finished my performance, I was asked to stay on a par-3 hole and hit a tee shot with each group that came through to try to help improve their score. When Yogi's group came through, he walked over to say hello and I told him that I was a big fan of the Yankees. A few minutes later, I hit my tee shot to within three feet of the hole. Yogi got very excited about this so I decided to ask him for his autograph. He said he would be happy to, so I handed him a ball with "The Dennis Walters Golf Show" logo on it and a Sharpie pen to write with. As he started to sign the ball, he seemed to be having some trouble. When he finished and handed the ball to me, he said, "Gee, Dennis, it's really hard to write on these pimples."

I laughed, of course, gave him a high five, and thanked him for making my day by presenting me with my very own "Yogi-ism."

* * *

The first time I appeared at the annual charity golf tournament that Fuzzy Zoeller puts on in New Albany, Indiana, baseball Hall of Famer George Brett was in the audience. During the question and answer session that's always a part of my show, Brett stepped out of the crowd.

"I want to hit one off the big tee," he said.

"Why sure, George," I said with a smile.

Many people, including several touring pros, have tried this shot over the years and most have met with failure. The tee is three feet high and much more difficult to hit a ball from than one would think. As I always did before I let someone try it, I demonstrated the correct way to hit the ball. My shot sailed a good 200 yards straight down the middle.

I figured as great a hitter as George was when he was playing for the Kansas City Royals, he by all rights should smash it right off the tee. First, though—since I'm a right-handed player—we had to get him a left-handed club. Fuzzy sent a volunteer up to the pro shop to get a left-handed driver out of the lost-and-found bin.

With a proper club firmly in his grasp, George strode toward the big tee as if he were "Casey at the Bat." Everybody, including me, was sure he would just murder the ball and send it into orbit. The anticipation in the audience was high as Brett carefully assumed his stance. He then swung with all his might and the audience, of course, expected the ball to be immediately airborne. However, he barely touched the top of the golf ball and it simply dribbled off the tee onto the ground. It actually looked like some kind of a trick shot, so I asked him if he was trying to replace me in my show. The remark received a pretty good laugh from the crowd.

Whenever people attempt this shot, they almost always swing too low and hit the tee instead of the ball. George was the opposite. He hit maybe two dimples on the top portion of the ball and it just toppled off the tee. That was actually tough to do, so I told him that it was one of the greatest shots I'd ever seen and I wanted him to teach me how to do it.

Determined to show the crowd that he could hit the ball as far as I had, George took three more swings. Each failed miserably and he never touched more than two or three dimples on the ball. It would wobble, then tumble off the tee and never roll more than a few inches. To my amazement, he never came close to touching the tee. That's how incredibly grooved his swing was. He hit the same spot on the ball every time. I thought that was pretty darn good and I told him so. When he finally gave up, George handed the club to me and I immediately saw that the metal head was bent out of shape because of the force of his swing and the fact that he had been contacting the ball with the hosel of the club. That driver went from the lost-and-found bin to the wastebasket.

Even though George was having a good laugh along with the rest of us (at his expense), I could tell that he was frustrated that he couldn't hit the ball. Fuzzy suddenly walked up carrying a plastic ball the size of a baseball and put it on the big tee. George grabbed the damaged club again, whirled around, took a Herculean swing and launched the ball down the fairway. I mean he absolutely killed it. Smiling broadly, he turned to face the audience and raised both of his arms in a signal of victory.

*   *   *

I loved baseball when I was young and enjoyed going to the major league parks to watch games. Since many major league baseball players are avid golfers, I had the idea that it would be fun to do my golf show at a major league baseball park some day. I sent letters to all of the major league baseball clubs, but all I got back were rejections. The reasons ranged from a golf show not fitting into an organization's plans, to not having any money, or that it had never been done before and it was hard for them to see the value. All were lame excuses as far as I was concerned.

One day, though, I finally got a positive response from the California Angels. I was already scheduled to do a show in Los Angeles so the opportunity to do one in Anaheim fit perfectly in our travel plans. The night before I was to appear at the ballpark, Dad and I were invited to watch the Angels play. Arriving with Muffin in tow, we were ushered to one of the team's owner's suites. We saw quite a few celebrities. One of them was then Vice President George Bush, who watched the game from a nearby suite.

Dinner was provided before the game. For dessert, we had ice cream sundaes that were served in miniature Angels' batting helmets. After I ate my sundae, I asked my father to wash out my little helmet. I then put it on Muffin's head. It fit perfectly and she wore it the rest of the game.

The next morning I was scheduled to tape a TV show hosted by Roy Firestone. It was for an ESPN series called "The Sports Look." Sharing the same studio, oddly enough, was a program called "The People's Court." The star of that show was the famous Judge Wapner. At one point, Roy and I were out in the hallway talking when Judge Wapner walked out of his dressing room. When we were introduced, I asked Judge Wapner if he would mind having his photo taken with Muffin and me. He kindly agreed, and then held Muffin while I stood next to him using my crutches. After the picture was taken, the judge set Muffin on the floor. When he straightened up, however, he noticed that the black robe he was wearing was covered with white dog hair! Boy, I never saw anyone get that upset over a "few" dog hairs.

Following my interview with Roy, I went to the ballpark to go over the logistics for my show and to have a short practice session. Originally, the plan was for me to hit balls from home plate. So when I got to the stadium, I met with the groundskeeper to discuss the details. Listen, I had always known that golf course superintendents could sometimes be tough, but this baseball guy was *ruthless*. He told me in no uncertain terms what I could and could not do.

"You park your golf cart over by the dugout, you come in along the dirt in front of the dugout, and you go up the little path right by home plate. You *do not* drive on home plate and you *do not* drive on the grass."

He also made it clear that I was to hit from the right side of the batter's box and *not* from home plate. He was adamant about it. And there was more.

"You go on at 7:05," he said. "If you aren't off by 7:23, we're *taking* you off."

After Mr. Congeniality left, I noticed that the dirt was really hard in the area where he wanted me to hit from. So hard, in fact, that it was difficult to push a golf tee into the ground. Near home plate, though, the ground was much softer and it was very easy to stick in a tee.

I decided at that moment that no matter what the groundskeeper had said, I was going to conduct my show near home plate where the ground was softer. Just as I was finishing up my practice session, Angels manager Doug Rader came out of the dugout carrying his golf clubs. "C'mon, Dennis," he said. "Let's hit some drivers."

It was great. We set up near the dugout and began hitting regulation golf balls way up into the bleachers. When fans arrived at the game that night, a lot of them found my logoed Maxfli's under their seats. Although I had used regular golf balls during my practice session, for the show that night I used "Cayman" balls because they only travel half the distance of regular golf balls. The balls were developed for use in the Cayman Islands because land space is hard to come by and they aren't able to have regulation-size golf courses. My reason for the change in equipment was to enable me to tee off from home plate and safely use my driver, thus allowing me to hit all of my trick shots. If I had used regular balls, the longest club I could have hit would have been my 7-iron. Real golf balls flying into a bleacher full of fans would not have been good.

As I went by the dugout to start my show that night, I looked around to see if the groundskeeper was anywhere in sight. He wasn't, so I drove right over the grass and began hitting balls from the side of home plate. If the groundskeeper saw me from somewhere in the stadium, I'm sure he was not a happy camper.

For me, the highlight of the whole show was when they put Muffin's face on the Jumbo-tron TV screen, still wearing the little

Angels batting helmet on her head. Her face lit up the whole screen and 33,000 fans went absolutely crazy.

As mentioned earlier, I always invite a spectator to try to hit one off the big tee and this night was no exception. The first "volunteer" was Angels outfielder Chili Davis. He was actually a good golfer, but he missed as most people do. The other Angels then pushed rookie Dante Bischette out of the dugout. It quickly became clear that Dante was not a golfer. He was an excellent hitter, however, so I figured he might be able to connect off the big tee. As a general rule, good athletes who have never played golf have a better chance of hitting the ball off the three-foot tee than those who play regularly. Good golfers tend to swing underneath the ball. Dante took a wild rip at it and missed. That ticked him off so he grabbed the golf club like he was holding a baseball bat and got ready to try it again. What he hadn't noticed, though, was that my dad had switched the Cayman ball on the big tee and replaced it with one of our exploding talcum powder balls. When he was ready, Dante took another ferocious swing and this time made perfect contact with the ball. Talcum powder flew everywhere, and it was the biggest mess you have ever seen. The other Angels and the spectators howled with laughter and I can only imagine the look on the poor groundskeeper's face when he saw his beautiful green grass covered with white powder.

Dante was kind of heartbroken after my dad told him about the golf ball switch. When he came over to shake my hand before heading back to the dugout, he whispered, "Don't tell anybody that it was a fake ball, Dennis. I want my teammates to think I'm so strong that I broke it."

A year later, the Atlanta Braves invited me to do a show. The team was one of the doormats of the National League at the time but I didn't care. My goal was to appear at as many baseball stadiums as I could, so I considered myself lucky to be able to perform at Fulton County Stadium. Because of the team's dismal record, it was difficult getting fans to come to the games. Only about 3,000 people were in the stands the night of my show and it made the stadium feel like a vast, empty box. I felt better, though, when I saw that my old friend Joe Inman and his son were in the seats behind home plate. I knew then that it would be a fun night.

With my golf cart parked between home plate and first base, I began my routine with the Cayman balls. I hit everything toward centerfield and watched as they rolled to the outfield wall. After I hit my blindfold shot with the driver, I heard wild cheering even before I got my mask off. I then saw that several fans were waving towels and pointing to the outfield wall as if I had smashed a home run. My dad informed me then that my drive had gone 10 or 15 yards farther than my previous shots and had flown over the outfield fence. I had hit my first major league round-tripper.

After completing the show to rousing cheers, I drove my golf cart around on the warning track toward a door in the outfield wall that was used to bring in large maintenance vehicles. As usual, Muffin was in the seat beside me. Uncharacteristically, as we neared the warning track, she jumped off the cart and promptly took a pee right there in the outfield. The next year, the Braves won the National League pennant. I like to think that it was because Muffin had "anointed" Fulton County Stadium that night.

* * *

Believe it or not, I have also done my show at the Metrodome in Minneapolis in the middle of February. This time it was an appearance at the Great Minnesota Golf Show. Upon my arrival, I was told that the outfield bleachers would be closed off to spectators. This caused me to decide to use regular golf balls for the performance instead of the Cayman balls. After arranging my cart near third base, I began rocketing shots into the outfield seats. At one point in the show, a spectator directed my attention to a large banner for Coca-Cola that was hanging from the rafters above the bleachers. The guy then asked me if I thought I could hit the sign with a ball. Feeling a bit cocky because I had been hitting the ball so well, I replied, "Which letter?"

"The O in 'Cola,'" he said with a smile.

On the very next shot—to the audience's amazement as well as my own—I hit the O in "Cola"—dead center.

That was *very* cool.

*　　*　　*

In the years after my accident—knowing that I was a big baseball fan—my great friend (and former Yankee) Ralph Terry often took me to the Old Timers Game at Yankee Stadium. He also took me into the locker room and got to be pretty good at maneuvering me around in my wheelchair. Among the many Yankee greats that I was thrilled to meet were Mickey Mantle, Whitey Ford, and Joe DiMaggio.

During one of those outings to the ballpark I was able to bring along my friend John Cafone. John was the golf pro who had made my golf clubs and he was a diehard Yankee fan. Well, the moment Ralph told all the Old Timers that John was a teaching pro he was suddenly giving golf lessons to all of his childhood heroes. That night, it was as good as it gets.

Unfortunately, another night with one of the Old Timers wasn't so good. I had been invited to do a show for the Italian American Club at Bonaventure Country Club near my Florida home and I was ecstatic about it because one of the attendees was to be Joe DiMaggio. My hope, if I had the chance, was to get the "Yankee Clipper" to sign something for my buddy Wayne.

At the banquet that night, I saw that DiMaggio was sitting by himself so I decided to go over and say hello. I had a brand new American League baseball with me, and I had brought Joe a goody bag with a dozen of my logoed golf balls and a "Dennis Walters Golf Show" tee shirt.

Coming up to where DiMaggio was sitting, I said, "Hi, Joe. I'm Dennis Walters, a friend of Ralph Terry's. We met once at Yankee Stadium." After he returned my greeting, I told him that I had some golf balls for him and gave him the bag. I then asked if he would mind autographing a ball for a friend.

Well, folks, the guy went absolutely ballistic.

"All you want is my signature," he said angrily. "And these golf balls are nothing but a bribe. You guys are all alike."

At first, I was shocked by his outburst. Then I got mad. I told him what I thought he should do with his signature and then I left.

If you ask me, Joe DiMaggio must have had the world's greatest publicity machine working for him because he was always portrayed as such a nice guy—when he really wasn't.

At least, that night he wasn't.

– *Chapter 20* –

Ever the Politician

IN THE EARLY 1990s, I was asked by the National Rehabilitation Hospital in Washington, D.C. to do a show at a charity event that was to be held at the TPC at Avenel in Potomac, Maryland. Little did I know that my contact person at the hospital would be a lady named Dorothy, the daughter of then President George Bush. Deep down I was hoping that the president would participate in one form or another at the golf tournament. I wanted to meet him.

As is often the case, I did my show before the event began. There was a great crowd on hand but not a sign of President Bush. I learned, though, that he would be a part of the awards presentation at the conclusion of play. Later, as I anxiously waited for the ceremony to start, I could see Secret Service personnel hard at work preparing the building for a presidential visit. When their inspection was complete and it was okay for people to enter the building, Muffin and I were at the front of the line. I grabbed a seat in the first row and sat there with Muffin on my lap. She was still in her show attire, which consisted of sunglasses and a visor. After President Bush finally arrived, he gave a short speech and then handed out prizes to the winners of the tournament. Following the ceremony, Dorothy escorted the president around the room and introduced him to people. Eventually, they came over to Muffin and me.

"Who do we have here?" he asked, reaching down to rub Muffin under her chin. Without missing a beat, I answered, "This is Muffin, and she is a good little Republican."

Dorothy then introduced me to her father. As you might imagine, I desperately wanted to get a photo of Muffin with the president for her album. I didn't think I should ask for one with me as well, so I decided to let Muffin have the honor.

"Mr. President," I asked, "would you mind if I took a picture of you and my dog?"

"Of course, of course," he replied graciously. "I would love to have my picture taken with this loyal Republican."

Before the opportunity could vanish, I handed Muffin to the president and quickly snapped three pictures of them with my camera. Muffin rarely looked directly into a camera, and I think it was because the flash scared her. This time, however, perhaps because she had her sunglasses on, she looked directly at me. One of the photos that I took that day turned out to be absolutely the best picture ever taken of Muffin, and probably the best picture ever taken of a smiling George Bush. (Later, I had an 8x10 made of it and sent it to the White House.)

After the president moved on to the next group, two things happened that made a great day even better. First, a man walked over to me and handed me a card, saying that he worked with the official White House photographer. He instructed me to fill out the card with my name, address, where I saw the president, and what time my photo was taken and what I was wearing. He then said, "In about six months, you'll receive a copy of the photo that was taken of you with the president." By that, I assumed he meant he'd snapped a picture of Muffin and me when I was talking to the president. Much to my surprise, however, the photo that eventually arrived was of me taking the photos of *them*. I was thrilled to have it and it was soon hanging on my wall of fame.

The second exciting thing that happened that day was that we also got to meet the first lady. During the awards ceremony, Mrs. Bush had sat quietly off to the side of the room. But being the dog lover that she was, she couldn't resist eventually coming over to pet Muffin.

She said to me, "And who might this be?"

"Her name is Muffin," I said. I then repeated my line about her being a Republican.

In the short time we spoke, I found Mrs. Bush to be a lovely woman who was very easy to talk to. At one point, I told her about a bumper sticker that I had recently seen. "It said, 'The more I see of people, the more I love my dog.'"

"True, true," the first lady replied. "But don't quote me on that, Dennis."

Believe me, it was a thrilling day that I won't forget.

*   *   *

During the mid-1990s I had another memorable government-related experience. I got a call one day and was told that Senator Orrin Hatch of Utah wanted me to perform at a golf event in Park City that was being held to raise money to benefit Utah Family Charities. It was the kind of organization that I enjoyed helping, so I was very interested in making the trip. That is, if Mulligan and I could get there.

Ever since I had been traveling with my pets, I'd only flown on airlines that allowed me to bring them on board in approved pet carriers. I never considered flying with them in the cargo compartments. My schedule had already been set when I received the invitation to go to Park City, so I told the tournament director that I would have to see if I could get the necessary connections.

"Not going to be a problem," she said. "I'll send you first class tickets on Delta."

Politely, but firmly, I said, "I won't fly with Delta. I'll make my own arrangements on another airline."

"You seem pretty adamant about this," she said. "You must've had a bad experience."

"Not at all," I replied. "I like Delta. But apparently they had problems with pets in the past. They won't let me keep my dog in the cabin and I absolutely refuse to put her in the belly of the plane." The way I looked at it, they had their rule and I had mine. The tournament director said she understood, but that she would get back to me soon.

Shortly thereafter she called to say that all of the arrangements were made and she had cleared things with Delta so that Mulligan could ride in her pet carrier in the first class cabin. The only stipulation she made was that I was not to tell any of the other passengers that I had a dog aboard. I told her that I needed that in writing, because I knew that as soon as I got to the airport somebody was going to hassle me about the dog.

"Believe me," she said, "everything is taken care of but we can't put this in writing because it is against every policy that Delta has."

"Well, then," I said, "I guess you'd better tell me how we're going to pull this off."

It turned out that Salt Lake City was one of Delta's hubs and Senator Hatch had been instrumental in helping Delta get this accomplished. The tournament director said that when I got to the airport in Memphis (where I was performing before heading to Utah) I should check in at Delta and look for a supervisor wearing a red jacket. Once I found this supervisor and told him who I was, everything would be taken care of.

Sure enough, when I arrived at the Memphis airport the Delta folks were waiting for me and asked if I had my special cargo. I pointed to the black mesh duffel bag that I had with me and said, "She's right in here."

One of the Delta employees said, "You know, I've been working for Delta for a long time and I've never seen anything like this before. It must have taken an Act of Congress."

"Actually," I replied with a chuckle, "it was just the Senate."

The flight to Utah was one of the smoothest and most enjoyable that I had ever had. On top of that, Senator and Mrs. Hatch were wonderful hosts and I ended up participating in the tournament several more years. In the months following that first event, I took advantage of my special arrangements and flew on Delta a few more times. Partly as a result of Mulligan's exemplary behavior during those trips, Delta changed its policy the following year and began to allow pets to once again fly in the cabin with their owners. My sister Barbara and I refer to this as the "Mulligan Law."

*   *   *

One year, at Senator Hatch's tournament, Muhammad Ali was the honored guest. It turned out that we were staying at the same hotel, so arrangements were made for Mulligan and me to visit with Ali in his room. Naturally, Mulligan did her tricks for him and he returned the favor by showing us some of his magic tricks. The funniest thing about the whole experience was that after he did his tricks, he showed us how he did them. For example, he placed a scarf in his hand and made it disappear. After we applauded to show our appreciation, he then slipped off a fake thumb where the scarf had been placed. And it seemed to me that he got an even bigger kick out of that than actually performing the tricks. It was unbelievable! Mulligan and me, all alone with Muhammad Ali.

He is—and it was—the greatest.

– Chapter 21 –

A Day in the Life . . .

I LEAD WHAT I WOULD CALL a very boring life. Not boring in terms of the people I meet or the places I visit, but boring in the fact that there's a sameness to my life that I don't change very much. I actually have two lives. One life when I'm on the road, and one when I'm at home.

I'm usually on the road from mid-April to the beginning of November. The only constant during this period is that I wake up and go to sleep each night in a different city. What happens in between is anything but typical. Each day is different, and that is what helps make the six months go extremely fast. I schedule between 80 to 100 shows for a typical year, which doesn't give me much time to relax. Maybe 25 to 30 of those shows are performed in the early spring or after I return home in the fall. The rest take place during my incredibly busy summer tour. It all works out well. By the time I'm tired of traveling, it's time to come home. Just about when I get sick of being at home, it's time to go on the road. I jokingly say that I follow the birds, heading south in the winter and north in the summer.

My days at home in Florida usually begin about 8 a.m. The kind of mood that I'm in on a particular day depends on the type of night that I had. If I have had an especially vivid dream about my playing golf or running on the beach, the stark reality of my situation when I awaken can put me in a somber mood. I try to shake this off as quickly as I can and focus only on the present.

My mornings are almost always the same. The first thing that I have to do is to empty my bladder. I sleep with an external catheter attached to a drainage bag. My bladder continually empties itself during the night, but before I start moving in the morning I must be sure that my bladder is completely emptied. While I'm attempting to complete this task, Benji Hogan, who spends the night sleeping at the foot of my bed, is either awake already or just beginning to stir. Now it's time for him to empty his bladder—or his "tank," as I refer to it. Because of a problem he had when he was neutered, Hogan has the world's smallest bladder and if I don't get him outside pretty darn quick, an accident is just waiting to happen. I have often thought about checking to see if a night drainage bag was available for dogs.

In order for me to get out of bed in the morning, I push down hard on my right elbow in order to prop myself up. This helps me get my balance and then I start shimming on my butt over to my wheelchair, which is parked on the right side of my bed. I slide onto the chair and then, one by one, grab hold of my legs. Since they are dead weights, I have to use both of my hands to lift them one at a time and carefully put them on the footrest of the wheelchair. If they are not balanced just right they may slip off, and because I have no feeling in them, I might roll over them with the chair. Once I am all set in the chair, Benji Hogan jumps on my lap and we head out of the bedroom. I have to "pop a wheelie" to get down the one small step that leads to the screened-in porch. I then open the porch door and let Hogan out. He does what he has to and is back inside in record time. This whole procedure takes about 20 minutes. Compare that to the time that it takes you to get up, go to the bathroom and then go back in your room. Five minutes, maybe?

Once Hogan is back inside, he is relentless in his pursuit of breakfast. Again, I follow a daily routine. I feed him and make sure he has water. When he's finished eating, I ask, "Have you burped yet?" With that he lets out a large belch. It's now my turn to eat. With food out of the way for both of us, I start my morning phone calls.

I have a lot more going on behind the scenes than the public imagines, much like advance work for anyone in the entertainment business. The perception, probably, is that I arrive to do a show, hit golf balls for an hour, pack up my clubs and go on to the next event. It's a lot more involved than that! During the winter, I have to get my schedule for the upcoming year organized. Believe me, trying to plan a hundred events all over the country is not easy. Each event requires several phone calls before getting a confirmed date. Once I have the date, I then have to go over my list and see what is scheduled the day before and the day after. I also have to determine if I can drive to an event or if I need to fly. If I need to fly, I have to make sure that I can get a flight that will get me to the event on time—and I have to do that *before* I make my final commitment to put on a show. If I can drive, I have to calculate the distance and time and make sure it is doable. Once I finish making my morning calls, I catch up on correspondence, check e-mails and, in between, talk to people who are returning my calls. This daily routine usually takes three or four hours.

Since I don't have an agent, my sister helps me book the shows and work out the travel details. It's not easy. I have often wondered if it would lessen our workload to have an agent make all of the arrangements, but I always concluded that no one could do a better job than Barbara and I. Frankly, I'm ambivalent about agents. Years ago, when I felt strongly that I needed one to help me get started, I couldn't get any agents to even talk to me about it. The larger agent organizations, such as IMG, Pro's Incorporated, and Cornerstone Sports, all turned me down. It was devastating at the time, but now I'm glad that it happened. My father went by the philosophy that if you want something done right, you had to do it yourself. Through trial and error, we succeeded in booking shows, obtaining sponsorships, and organizing our tour.

All of this detail work is time-consuming and tiring. Another one of my dad's favorite sayings was, "You can't run a car without gas." So, around noon, I have something to eat. Following lunch, it's time to take a shower and get dressed. My house has been set up to be wheelchair friendly so I can roll from room to room without any problems. The shower is very large and it has a built-in bench that's the same height as my wheelchair. That makes it really easy for me to get out of the chair and onto the bench. After my shower, I spend the next 20 minutes putting on my braces and clothes. (Before my accident, I was the world's fastest dresser. It was mostly because I would sleep until the last minute and then jump into my clothes and shoes and off I'd go. Boy, do I miss being able to do that. I know things are not going to change. But if I had a wish list, being able to get myself ready in a hurry would be near the top of the list.)

Once I'm dressed, I head to the golf course to either practice or play a few holes. I live off the ninth hole of the Jacaranda Golf Club in Plantation, Florida. It has been home to me for the past 26 years. I have my golf cart in the garage and Benji and I drive through a small park to get to the course. Many years ago the superintendent built a small practice tee for me on the back of the range so I could practice by myself and work on my routine. The tee has since been enlarged and trees have been planted to provide shade.

I spend a lot of my time there. Usually, I practice two to three hours at a time. When I was younger I used to practice a lot longer. As I've gotten older, however, I've found that I can maintain my skills with less practice. I once asked golf psychologist Bob Rotella if this was a normal occurrence. Before he answered my question, he asked me how long I had been playing golf. "About 40 years," I replied. He then explained that as long as I was hitting the ball up to my standards, and I continued to improve and have fun, the knowledge that I had gained in those 40 years allowed me the luxury of cutting down the time I had been spending on the practice tee. He said that due to my busy schedule it was probably a positive thing, because it would allow me to avoid excess fatigue. His answers made me feel good about my routine.

Being able to practice my conventional shots without assistance gives me a great feeling of independence. I begin my practice session with stretching exercises and follow it up by hitting some short-irons just to loosen up. I then spend most of my practice time hitting drivers. By using a pair of giant chopsticks, I'm able to tee up a golf ball without any help. The chopsticks were a gift from the Hall of Fame golfer "Lighthorse" Harry Cooper. Whenever Harry was giving golf lessons, his bad back would give him trouble because he was constantly bending over to tee up balls. Thanks to the long chopsticks, Harry didn't have to bend over so much. Harry was working at Westchester Country Club in New York for my old boss Bob Watson. It occurred to him that the chopsticks would be useful to me, so he asked Bob to bring me a pair. Harry was right. The three-foot long chopsticks allow me to pluck a ball from the ground and place it on a rubber tee that is attached to a string. If the tee moves after the shot, I pull on the string and replace it in the proper spot and reach for another ball. I hit a lot of drivers because that's the swing I use on most of my trick shots.

I can do about 35 different trick shots, but basically I use the same swing. Some shots do require a slightly different swing, but it would be very difficult for me to change for each trick. I also feel that by practicing with my driver, which is my longest club, I'm stretching and building up my muscles to their fullest. When I switch from hitting just conventional shots and begin to work on my trick shots, I always have someone help me because this type of practice is much more involved and I do need aid in setting up the shots. This is also a good way for my assistant and me to rehearse what we will actually do during a show.

Jacaranda Golf Club has two courses: the East and the West. The West course is shorter and tighter, and my favorite holes are the front nine there. On a normal day, I will break 40 for nine holes. The lowest score I have ever shot for nine holes, playing from my cart, is 32. That day I won $18. Not bad considering the original bet was for $2. The lowest score I ever had before my accident was 63, which I shot in college. I have also had four holes in one—two standing and two sitting.

Often near the end of the day, when Jacaranda is no longer crowded, I like to go out to the second hole of the East course and test equipment and practice hitting my driver. I hit drivers from about 50 yards in front of the green back toward the tee. It's a very flat area that's framed by trees on the right and houses on the left. I have measured the distance of this "practice range" to be about 225 yards. If I hit a good drive, under normal conditions, I can reach the rough 225 yards away. On occasion, I can hit it 10 to 15 yards further.

Late afternoon is my favorite time of day. The pink and orange sunsets are magnificent, and the wild green parrots that are common to south Florida are amazing to watch as they settle into the trees. Their brilliant color and loud chirping make them easy to spot.

The entire time that I am practicing or playing, Benji Hogan is right beside me on the golf cart. The moment I start for home, however, he jumps off the cart for his daily run on the course. I usually let him run for about nine holes. As soon as his run begins, he looks for what I call his "treasure sticks." A treasure stick can be a stick of any size, from a twig to a large palm frond. If the first stick he picks up is small, he will be on the lookout for a larger one and as soon as he spots one he will trade up for a larger model. He is totally unhappy unless he is carrying a stick. As we leave the golf course and head for home through the park, I tell him he has to drop the stick. He always leaves it in the same place and now has a pile high enough to start a bonfire. On some occasions, I let him run on the driving range. If this is the case, instead of picking up sticks, he picks up golf balls. The most he has held in his mouth at one time is three—that's his record! The sight of Benji Hogan running on the golf course never fails to bring a smile to my face.

Whenever I play a round of golf my goal is to have fun and not get frustrated. I don't play from the back tees. The course I play is usually around 6,000 yards because that allows me to use different strategies on each hole. If I played the course any longer, I would have to hit a fairway wood into many of the greens and it wouldn't be as much fun. Playing a shorter course allows me to challenge myself both mentally and physically, which is one of the beauties of the game. It is my opinion that is one of the biggest mistakes golfers make when playing away from home—playing from the wrong set of tees.

When I started to play golf again, the thing that bothered me most was knowing that I would never play as well as I did before my accident. I dwelled on that a lot. One day, though, I realized that I was looking at my performance in the wrong way. Instead of looking at how I used to play, I needed to look at how I was playing in the present. That became my starting point, and my goal was then to work toward improvement based on "today." Once this revelation sunk in, I began to see how much I had improved since starting to play golf again and I felt much better about my situation. I know it's not healthy to base your self-image on how good a golfer you are or on your accomplishments. In my case, though, my improved golf game had a tremendous positive effect on my self-worth. I suppose that happens when golf has been so much a part of a person's life. Golf helped me mentally because I was able to regain a great deal of my independence through the game. And once I began my career as a trick-shot artist, I felt even better about myself.

When I'm at home during the winter I usually play nine holes two or three times a week with friends at Jacaranda. Since I hit all of my full shots from the cart, the people at my shows assume that I drive my cart onto the green in order to putt. This is not the case. When I get to the green, I lock my braces and get up on my crutches. I hike over to the ball, balance myself on one crutch, and putt one-handed. I do the same thing when I'm in a bunker—a one-handed swing with my sand wedge. When I practice chipping and putting, Benji Hogan is a big help. I putt or chip the ball toward the cup and Hogan then retrieves the ball and brings it back to me. That way I can keep practicing and not use up all of my energy going back and forth getting the ball. We do the same thing when I practice my bunker shots. Hogan never fails to amaze me.

My pace of play is about equal to most amateur golfers, and I find that going nine holes is just enough. Getting up on my crutches is tiring. If I get out to putt five or six times in nine holes, it's a nice workout but not overly exhausting. On the other holes, I usually chip it up close enough for a gimme. Hogan then retrieves the ball for me. He is a huge help and he makes playing golf so much easier and fun for me.

I'm usually on the course until the sun starts to set and then I head for home. I put my cart back in the garage and go into the sanctuary of my home. After traveling so much during the summer months, it feels good to go into the house and look around at the things that I enjoy so much. I have a huge porcelain bird collection in the dining room, and the walls of the living room are covered with golf artwork. In my bedroom, I have memorabilia that I have been collecting for years. Some of it bears the signatures of several well-known celebrities.

I call it a day around 11 p.m. and hope that I will get a good night's sleep. In the morning, I do just about the same thing all over again. Even though I face enormous daily challenges in my personal life, I am quite pleased with my professional life. I know every day that I will be able to hit golf balls and that is the one thing I love to do most. In this regard, I consider myself to be fortunate.

But as I said earlier, I still consider much of my life to be boring.

– Chapter 22 –

More Stories

I HAVE ACCUMULATED quite a few stories in the 26 years that I have been performing. Some are more memorable than others, of course, but they all have a place in the scrapbook of my mind. In the early years, my dad and I kept a record of the funny incidents that happened (as well as where the best restaurants were across the country). But as the years went by, we just got too busy to keep it up. When we returned to Florida at the end of a tour, however, we would tell my mother and sister that year's best stories. Here are some of my favorites.

I'm often asked to reveal the most unusual thing that has ever taken place during one of my shows. For a long time, I never really had a good answer to that question. But finally something happened that was worthy. I was doing my show one year at the Senior PGA Tour event at the Silverado Resort in Napa, California. There was a nice crowd of close to 1,000 people on hand and things were going well. In the middle of my demonstration on how to hit a bunker shot, however, as I was telling the audience to be "aggressive," I noticed that almost everyone was looking at the other end of the range instead of at me. So I looked, too, and what I saw were two golfers fighting. I mean, it was a regular brawl. The two men were rolling on the ground like a couple of kids. *Look at those clowns,* I thought to myself. *Fighting during my show.* It was at that moment that I realized that the two men were Senior Tour players J.C. Snead and Dave Hill. When fellow players and onlookers finally broke up the fight, the much bigger J.C. had his foot on Dave's throat. Unfortunately for Dave, J.C. was still wearing his golf shoes—with steel spikes!

A few minutes later I resumed my show, picking up where I had left off. After reminding the audience that they needed to be aggressive with a bunker shot, I also cautioned them not be as aggressive as J.C. and Dave. A few weeks later, *Sports Illustrated* mentioned the fight and that it had occurred during one of my shows. Later that same week, the late Hans Kramer of International Management Group (IMG), the company that had run the Senior PGA event, called me and said, "You really know how to make your show interesting."

* * *

One year I went to Penn State University to conduct a show for the school's Professional Golf Management program. It's a program offered to students who want to work in the golf industry. The students were going to put on a tournament for amputee golfers so they asked me if I would conduct a clinic. For as long as I've been doing my show, I've rarely had more than one or two rainouts per year, and I consider that a pretty good record. The one at Penn State, however, had a strong possibility of being rained out because it was absolutely pouring that day. I hated the thought of not doing it, so Barbara and I put on rain suits and went out to the range to see if there was anything we could do to salvage the day. Since a luncheon was to be served later in the day, two large tents had been erected. There was an open area between the tents, so I decided that I would park my cart there and do the show while the audience was nice and dry beneath the tents.

To keep Benji and my clubs from getting wet, we kept them under one of the tents. I then went ahead and did my show in the rain. Barbara would get me a club, tee up a ball, and run back under the tent. It worked pretty well, actually, and I ended my show with a bit of advice for the amputee golfers. I told them that it wasn't too bad playing in the rain, except that they'd have to be careful not to rust. There were a couple hundred people in attendance and I think every one of them came up to me after the show to thank me for not canceling.

* * *

The first show I ever did with Chi Chi Rodriguez was at the Canon Greater Hartford Open. It was a very hot and humid day but the bleachers were full. Chi Chi asked me to go on first so I did. Every shot I hit was pure, the audience laughed at all my jokes and they gave me a standing ovation when I was finished. Before Chi Chi performed there was a short intermission. By the time the break was over, about 90% of the gallery had left. Chi Chi did his portion for the remaining few, then came over to tell me what a great job I had done. He then added with a laugh, "The next time we do a show together, Dennis, I'm going first." We've done six or seven shows since, and Chi Chi has always gone first. That was one of my dad's favorite stories and he never got tired of telling it.

* * *

I was at the old Roy Clark Celebrity Classic one year, and while it's unusual for me to actually play in one of these tournaments, I agreed to it this time. I was invited to be one of the "celebrities" in a four-man scramble format. Because I had not done my show first, my teammates didn't know who we were when Barbara and I arrived at our starting hole in my cart. I introduced myself and told them that I was "their group leader." I could see that this definitely did not thrill them. I told them that if it was all right with them, I would hit the first shot. Barbara winked at me as she teed up a ball. Our first hole was a par 3 and I proceeded to hit my tee shot to within 15 feet of the cup. My teammates were only moderately impressed . . . until each of them hit their shots into the lake by the green—then they liked my shot a lot more. When I went up on my crutches and knocked in the birdie putt, my teammates began to warm up to me. On the next hole, when I dropped a 40-footer for an eagle, those guys suddenly became my best friends. From then on, we had a fabulous time and finished in third place. As I mentioned, I don't get to play in many events like that. But it was so much fun that I wouldn't mind doing it more often.

*   *   *

Corporate events are fun stops on my tour. Every year John Perner of the Pepsi-Cola Company invites me to the outing that they put on during the PGA Championship. Instead of doing a show, I visit with the participants on the range and give them tips for improvement. During the outing, I stay on a par-3 hole and hit a ball with each group to try to help their score. One year I hit two balls for each group because Barbara had suggested that I try to hit a second shot off of a Pepsi can. It was a huge success, and more often than not the Pepsi can shot ended up closer to the hole. Maybe I'm on to something!

The Pepsi outing is always held on a course that's near the site of that year's PGA Championship. When it's over, everyone goes back to the corporate tent on the tournament course for dinner and "Casino Night." It's always a fun outing and I look forward to it every year.

I'm hoping that perhaps one year the PGA of America will ask me to take part in the annual Champions Clinic that's held at the event. That would be fun, too.

*   *   *

At another corporate outing one year, this one for the Illinois Tobacco and Candy Association at the Rail Golf Club in Springfield, Illinois, I was again stationed on a par-3 hole. My dad was teeing up the ball for me that day, and at one point needed to take a bathroom break. A tournament official picked him up in a cart and they headed for the clubhouse. Halfway there, someone called the official on his radio and said that one of the golfers had made a hole in one. My dad immediately said to the official, "It has to be Dennis." Apparently, he just had a feeling that it was me and he was right. My first thought after making the ace was, *Gee, that white Lincoln over there that's the prize for a hole in one sure is nice. But I wonder if I can get it in gray?*

When the tournament director came around to congratulate me, I asked him if I could change the color. "Read the fine print in your contract, son," he said. "You're not eligible."

The organizers of the event were nice enough to pay me an extra five hundred dollars, which somewhat helped ease the pain of the "lost" Lincoln.

* * *

The Bears Stern Stock Brokerage Company once invited me to do an outing at Wing Foot Golf Club in Mamaroneck, New York, the famed site of four U.S. Opens and a PGA Championship. I did my show and then went to stay on the 10th hole on the West course. This hole is a par 3 and is always ranked as one of the toughest in the country. Directly behind the 10th green is a home, and legend has it that during the 1959 U.S. Open, Ben Hogan always tried to hit his shot on line with the living room of the house. If he suc-ceeded, his ball would land safely in the middle of the green. I played the 10th hole 36 times that day and each time tried to take the same line as Mr. Hogan. Using a 3-wood, I was able to hit the green 26 times out of 36.

The caddie yard at Winged Foot is near the 10th hole and many of them were watching and cheering me on as I hit my shots. One time, I even hit the flagstick. Although I had several other close shots, I thought my performance was rather mediocre considering how many times I missed the green. Later, inside the clubhouse, I was able to take a look at Bobby Jones's scorecards from the 1929 U.S. Open. When I saw that he had bogeyed the 10th hole three out of four rounds, it made me feel a lot better about my performance that day. If the legendary Bobby Jones had trouble with it, the 10th was one tough hole.

* * *

One time a reporter from a TV station in Miami came out to my home course, Jacaranda Golf Club, to do a story on me. With the camera rolling, I started hitting shots and went through my bag of tricks. At one point during the interview he asked me if I could do any *really* unusual shots and I asked him to give me an example.

He said, "How about if we put a ball on the toe of my shoe, balance an egg on the ball, then you try to hit the ball without breaking the egg?

I did a similar shot in my show but it wasn't off someone's shoe, so this was a new twist. Not wanting to hit the reporter's foot, I swung a little high the first time that I tried it and splattered the egg all over him. On the second try, we succeeded. When I asked him not to show the first shot on television, he promised that he wouldn't. Not too surprisingly, the splattered egg shot led off the TV station's sports report that night.

* * *

On the way to a show a few years ago, Barbara and I were cruising down the Pennsylvania Turnpike in our motor home. I was driving and she was sleeping on the couch. Our beautiful Newmar Mountain Aire motor home was equipped with hand controls that were installed by an independent company and were very easy for me to use. The procedure was simple—pull back on the handle for the accelerator, push forward for the brake. I was doing about 60 miles an hour at the time, but decided to slow down a bit even though there weren't any other cars near me. As I began to apply pressure for the brakes, the entire apparatus let loose and came off the steering column. I could neither brake nor accelerate and was just sitting there with the handle in my hand. I immediately yelled for Barbara (I'm pretty sure I said, "We're in deep shit!"). As fast as she could, Barbara got down on the floor and used her hands to try and pump the brakes. It wasn't easy, but eventually we were able to guide the motor home over to the side of the road and stop it. It was truly scary. Soon after it happened, I had a flashback to my accident and it took me a long time to get my heart rate back to normal. The only good that came from that experience was that Barbara had to do all of the driving until we were able to get the hand controls fixed.

*   *   *

In 1978, when I was still in the early stages of my new career, I decided that if my story could get more exposure it would help me book additional shows. One day, out of the blue, I got a call from someone on the television show, "That's Incredible." The person had heard about me somewhere and asked if I would like to appear on the program. I agreed, and then told my dad that it was the break I'd been hoping for because the viewing audience was in the millions and I was sure we would get a ton of bookings after I did the program. A while later a TV crew came to my house in Florida and spent three days filming both at the house and at Jacaranda. Things went so well, in fact, that my dad and I were eventually invited to go to Hollywood and appear live with the show's hosts—Fran Tarkenton, John Davidson, and Kathy Lee Crosby. I was very excited about the trip and was certain that we would be picked up at the airport in a limo and then put up at the Beverly Hills Hotel. I could almost see my dad and me sitting at the pool with a bunch of movie stars. I said, "Dad, we've got it made." Boy, was I wrong.

When we got off the airplane in California, we saw a man in the terminal holding a sign that had "That's Incredible" and my name on it. We went over and introduced ourselves, and then I asked him where the limo was parked.

"You guys wait here while I go get the van," he said.

My *limo* turned out to be a rickety van without any seats in the back. My dad had to sit on the two wooden crates that held my portable seat and its attachments. As we drove out of the airport, I asked the driver if we could stop at the hotel before we went to the studio. "Sure," he said. "Next stop, Days Inn."

Obviously, we didn't see any movie stars at our hotel.

After we got to the studio, we learned that their plan was to show the film that they'd taken of me in Florida and then do a live interview. They wanted me to hit a shot or two, so they brought a golf cart onto the stage. There was also a planned "spectacular finale" to the segment, so it was suggested that I hit a ball out of host John Davidson's mouth. If you're familiar with what John looked like at the time, you know that he had one beautiful set of white teeth. To say that I was a tad bit nervous about doing the stunt is an understatement. Worse yet, they weren't going to tell John about the "finale" in advance; they were just going to spring it on him. When it was time for me to come on stage, I drove out in my golf cart and met the hosts. I then hit a few plastic golf balls into the audience. To set the stage for my shot out of John's mouth, Fran Tarkenton asked me to try a new trick shot he called the "watermelon shot." I had been told in advance that they were going to tee up a ball on a watermelon, but I was supposed to miss the ball and smash the melon as a gag. Then, with John standing there, Fran was going to say that the producers decided that they wanted John to become a human golf tee.

When everything was all set, Fran teed up a ball on a watermelon. I took a mighty swing and, as planned, missed the ball and hit the fruit. Watermelon went everywhere, as you might imagine. Fran, John, and Kathy Lee, who was wearing a beautiful white dress, were covered with seeds. The first four rows of the audience got splattered, too.

Fran then said, "Gee, that just didn't come off quite right."

To which I replied, "I'm only human and every now and then I miss one."

At that point, Fran persuaded a petrified John Davidson to lie on his back in front of me with a golf tee in his mouth. After a plastic ball was set on the tee, I took two waggles, swung away and proceeded to hit a perfect shot into the audience that flew over the "That's Incredible" sign. John remained on the floor for a few moments, then got up and shook my hand. I can tell you that his face was white as a ghost. During a commercial break, he whispered to me that he had never been more scared in his life.

Even though the bookings did not roll in as I had hoped, I had a great time doing "That's Incredible." In fact, I still receive residual checks from that initial appearance even after all these years. Early on, the checks were usually for around $150. However, the last one I got was for $1.32. The stub noted that it was for a showing of the program in Bolivia, South America.

Many years later, in 1992, I was on the practice tee at the Kapalua Resort in Maui, Hawaii, and who do I see hitting balls but none other than Fran Tarkenton. I went over and said hello, and then reminded him that I was the guy who had hit a plastic golf ball out of John Davidson's mouth. When Tarkenton replied that he didn't remember the incident, I was flabbergasted. He forgot it?

Now, that's *really* incredible!

– Chapter 23 –

Golf Lessons

BY THE END OF 2001, I had done 24 clinics with Tiger Woods and his foundation. At each site Tiger always arrived before the throng of kids showed up, and he'd use this time to work on his game, or, in some instances, he'd do a photo shoot or film a commercial. If he practiced, it gave me a unique opportunity to observe his swing up close and maybe get an idea of what it takes to be the world's number one golfer. Tiger and I could also joke around a bit and talk about things that were important to us, such as fishing. This free time also gave Tiger a chance to ask Benji Hogan some questions in hopes of stumping the "little guy."

After his warm-up, Tiger would then give individual instruction to about 25 lucky kids. Following that would be a press conference for the media, and then came the exhibition portion of the day where Benji Hogan and I led off as Tiger's opening act. Tiger's dad, Earl, followed my performance with an inspirational speech, and then Tiger would wind up the day with a display of his incredible shot-making ability. The clinics were usually held for between three and five thousand invited guests in cities all across America.

At one of the clinics that we did in the summer of 2000, I noticed that Tiger was practicing a big "rope hook"—a high, curving shot that probably moved 30 yards from right-to-left. It was quite different from the normal shape of his shot, which was only a slight draw from right-to-left. When I asked him about this new shot, he explained that it was the kind of shape that he needed for his drive at the par-5 13th hole at Augusta National Golf Club, home of the Masters. To me, it was extraordinary that he would be practicing that shot a full nine months before the next Masters. I was certain that none of his rivals had this foresight.

In October of that year, I was in Atlanta to do a show at the Tour Championship at East Lake Country Club and saw Tiger practicing on the range. As I watched him, I saw that he was still working on the same shot that I had seen him practicing months before. Driving by in my cart on the way to do my show, Tiger waved me to a stop. When I mentioned that I could tell that he was still practicing for the 13th at Augusta, I was rewarded with that magnetic Tiger smile.

I can't tell you how impressed I was every time I saw Tiger practicing that particular shot. It demonstrated to me how well he prepares himself for major championships. When he went after the fourth consecutive major at the 2001 Masters, I knew firsthand that Tiger had been preparing for this event for months and months. Tiger used that shot on number 13 during the last round, and it was at a critical time when he really needed to pull it off. He did. Later, when he was presented with the green jacket that signified victory, I thought, *the thirteenth at Augusta. Way to go, Tiger.* From that point on, for me, that phrase stood for long-term planning, clear thinking, determination, and success.

That story about Tiger exemplifies one of the beautiful things about golf: No matter how good you are, you can always improve. It's a never-ending learning experience, and even if you play golf your entire life you still will not have all the answers. If you enjoy a challenge, golf is the game for you.

* * *

Like a lot of people, I have my own theories about what makes a good golf swing. That's not to say that I consider myself an expert on the swing or how it should be taught. Teaching golf for a living is an art form and I have tremendous respect for the professionals who have the skill and dedication. I do, however, consider myself an expert on my *own* swing.

What's it like to have my golf swing? Well, short of shooting your legs full of Novocain, I think you can simulate it by first sitting down in a chair. A simple straight-back kitchen chair will do. Now, put your feet on either side of the chair. To make it even more realistic, hold your legs an inch or two off the floor. If your feet are *on* the floor, you get some support from your lower body even though you are sitting down. When I sit, I get no support or leverage from my feet, legs, and hips. Zero. What I have to do, then, is keep my legs out of the way. So, with you positioned on a chair with your feet off the floor, you can now experience what it's like to be strictly an arms and hands player like me.

Tricky, isn't it?

Whether you play golf sitting down or standing up, in order to hit good shots on a consistent basis you must master certain fundamentals. Holding the club properly is important because it will enhance both your direction and distance. It will also make your shots more consistent. A good grip should have both hands working together so that you can square the clubface at impact. A good grip is the steering mechanism for your swing and greatly influences all the aspects and positions that take place during the swing. A key element in a good grip is the amount of pressure that you use to hold the club. I have found that using relatively less pressure is better than holding the club too tight. If your hands are properly placed on the club, you can hold the club lightly but still maintain control. If your hands are not working together, the opposing forces will cause you to hold the club too tight and that will cause tension in the arms and hands that will destroy your swing.

As for alignment, the first thing I had to learn when I started to play sitting down was how to park my golf cart correctly. Proper alignment is critical if you want to hit your shots at the target. As I approach my shot, I visualize where I think I should park the cart.

I make sure that I am parallel left of my target line. If you stand behind me my cart will appear to be pointed to the left, as in an "open" stance. My seat, however, is still square or parallel to my target line. All golfers should start from this position. My friend Gary Wiren, the noted golf instructor, uses me as an example to explain alignment to his students.

Placing the ball in the proper position in your stance influences the direction of the shot and the trajectory it has. If the ball is played from further back in your stance, it will come out low and toward the right. If it is played more forward in your stance, it will have a higher trajectory and be more to the left. Since I'm unable to adjust my stance, I must focus on a spot on the ground where I believe the club head will be square as it passes through that spot. I also have to factor in where I want the ball to start. When I have a clear picture in my mind that these two factors are correct, that is where I place my ball. Try to use this visualization technique to improve your alignment.

Golf is a game of balance, rhythm, and timing. One of the beautiful things about golf is that you don't have to be six-foot-three or weigh 200 pounds to play good golf. Balance is probably my biggest obstacle. The way I see it, for a person who is standing, the legs act as stabilizers and error correctors. They enhance your balance and allow you the luxury of being able to compensate for an incorrect move. I do not have this luxury because my balance point is determined, not by my legs, but by the strap around my waist that holds me securely in my seat. The higher the balance point the less stability I have. I have to swing the club in a very precise manner in order to maintain my balance. One other comment about the legs: After learning how to play sitting down, I now agree with those who believe the legs are *not* the primary power source for most golfers. In my opinion, the legs only contribute approximately 20 to 30% to a golfer's power.

Proper timing and tempo are two other factors that will help you to play well on a consistent basis. As my swing guru Wayne likes to say, "Good tempo (the pace you swing the club and the amount of effort that you use), creates good timing (the sequence of events that unfold during your swing)." I have always had good tempo in my swing. For some reason, my tempo is one of the few things that I can remember about the swing that I had when I played standing up. I find this weird because I really can't remember what that old swing felt like. I can picture my old swing in my mind, and I can remember the tempo, but I can't tell you what it was like to flex my knees at a certain angle or what it felt like to shift my weight properly. I miss those feelings a lot, and sometimes those memories are quite painful and sad.

Swing path and clubface position are two more things that affect every golf shot. The path on which you swing the club determines the initial direction of the ball, and the position that the clubface is in at contact determines the kind of spin that will be applied and where the ball will end up. A long time ago, Bob Toski told me a simple rule of thumb to follow and I have used his advice ever since. He said, "Swing where you want the ball to start, and face your club where you want the ball to finish." I think it's great advice and I suggest you try it.

On my forward swing, I like to feel as though I swing the club as close to the right, rear fender of my golf cart as I can. This ensures that I will approach the ball from *inside* the target line. I then swing *along* the target line, contact the ball, and continue my swing toward the right, front fender (inside again). Basically, I am swinging from fender to fender. Using this method, it is almost impossible for me to slice a ball. If you are a chronic slicer, try to picture a golf cart behind you and swing as I do from fender to fender. I'm sure this technique will work for you, too.

One final comment about the golf swing. There has been a constant debate among experts as to the best method for swinging a club. Does the body begin the motion of the arms, or do the arms begin the motion of the body? Here are my thoughts. I believe playing golf is a progression of small steps that have to be followed. The first step all good golfers master is learning to use their arms and hands correctly. Once you do this, you are on your way to becoming a good player. Most tour players today favor the body or big muscle swing. This is a great way to play, provided you are in relatively good shape, spend a lot of time practicing, and are fairly athletic. Most of the people that I see playing golf do not meet all three of these criteria. I *only* use my arms and hands and I still play excellent golf. What "touch" and "feel" that I have comes from my arms and hands, too. Not my hips. Therefore, it is my opinion that the average golfer would do well to consider the arm swing method of playing because it is an easy concept to grasp and an excellent way to play.

All of the fundamentals and techniques that I have talked about in this chapter are important and if you master them you will have a far better chance of improving your game. Keep your arms tension free, swing the club in a circle—half of the circle on the backswing, half of the circle on the forward swing—and remember to keep the center of your body relatively still. You can make the golf swing as complicated as you want, but most of you will play better golf and enjoy it more if you make it simple. Try it.

Finally, I think that a valuable lesson to be learned from my experience is that in golf, as in life, you must learn to adjust and compensate whenever it is necessary to achieve your dream.

– Chapter 24 –

Life Lessons

WHEN I FIRST TRIED to develop my show, I did it entirely for my own benefit. I put so much time and effort into my golf game that it helped me cope with everything that was happening in my life. As I got better and started to perform before audiences, I began to see that people were responding not only to my golf shots, but also to what I was actually saying. What I told them was that it had always been my dream to play on the PGA Tour. But after my accident it was impossible to accomplish that dream. Through hard work and perseverance, however, I was able to reach for a *new* dream. Encouraging others to strive for their dreams has always been a cornerstone of my show. A presentation not only of golf lessons, but life lessons, too—and I use my own life to show that you should never give up your dreams. If someone is willing to pay the price, success at almost anything can be achieved. This message is universal, appealing to the young and elderly, golfer and nongolfer, to those who have physical problems and those who don't. It's a message that I believe with all my heart and I think the audience can tell. My wish is for the members of my audience to leave with a smile and the motivation to make their own dreams come true.

I talk about other things in my show, too. I mention the joy and beauty of golf, of being out in the fresh air and sunshine, and life in general. For most of us, I hope, golf will be a 50-year-long project that offers the chance to spend quality time with old friends and make new ones as well. There are valuable lessons to be learned from the game. If you're a golfer, you have to learn to play by the rules, get along with others, learn to budget your time, work toward a goal, strive to improve and reach for excellence. The bottom line, in my opinion, is that golf is simply great fun.

As a result of my experience, I believe the game can provide wonderful therapy for people with disabilities. If physically challenged people can accomplish the seemingly impossible task of learning how to play golf, they can achieve positive results in other aspects of their lives as well. Golf is a great confidence booster and a social icebreaker, and I encourage everyone—the physically challenged and the able-bodied—to at least give it a try.

I have done some motivational speaking in the past and hope to do more of it in the future. I begin my presentation by showing my golf show video. I then tell the audience a little bit of my personal history, answer questions, and conclude the presentation by having Benji Hogan dazzle the audience with his math skills and knowledge of golf trivia. Incorporated in my speech is something I call the "Six P's in the Pod of Success." They are:

1. **Preparation**—Plan well and work on the basic fundamentals of your task and goal setting.
2. **Perspiration**—Work hard.
3. **Perseverance**—Hang in there no matter what, never giving up.
4. **Performance**—Always strive for excellence.
5. **Possibilities**—Never stop dreaming. With desire, you can accomplish anything.
6. **Pleasure**—Enjoy the journey and the effort.

I have learned so much about life that I feel it is my responsibility to pass this knowledge on to others. If I did nothing more than hit trick shots during my show, I would still feel very good about my profession and myself. However, having the opportunity to influence others in a positive way has given me enormous satisfaction and it has made my performing that much more rewarding. Almost every phase of my life has been shaped and changed by this game, but the one thing that has never wavered is my love for it. When I was young, golf gave me my dreams of championships. Now it makes me realize that I am the champion of my dreams.

– Chapter 25 –

The Real Heroes in My Life

MY FATHER, ARTHUR "Bucky" Walters, died on February 26, 2001 at the age of 86. My mother, Florence, died November 29, 2001, at the age of 82. After I was injured in 1974, my dad and mom abandoned all plans for a leisurely retirement and devoted themselves to making sure that I was able to live my life in the best possible way. Dad spent the rest of his life traveling with me, and when he could no longer travel he continued helping and encouraging me in everything I did. A perfect example of my dad's determination occurred in 1986 when he had to have triple bypass heart surgery. His doctors commanded, "Absolutely no more traveling." Naturally, he took their advice but waited 10 more years to do so.

On the road, Dad was a one-man promotional band. He always carried golf balls with my logo (and in later years those with both mine and my show dog Benji Hogan's) on them and he always had brochures in his back pocket with complete information about the golf show. I clearly remember one time when we were eating in a restaurant and apparently he made a very strong impression on a man seated nearby. The man had obviously been eavesdropping on our conversation but did not hear everything. He marched right up to Dad, with me sitting there, and said, "It's really nice of you to take that handicapped kid with you." He thought that my dad was the golfer. Dad did not miss a beat when he said, "You've got it wrong." Pointing to me he said, "That's the star of the show." After a short pause to set up the punch line, he concluded by saying, "he's the golfer, I'm the gofer."

My father and mother celebrated their 61st wedding anniversary on August 13, 2000. They met on a blind date in 1937. My dad, being the lady's man that he was, had another date scheduled later that same evening. However, once he set eyes on my mom, he never made it to the other date. Dad and Mom were married in 1939, and at the time of their marriage my dad was a bookkeeper for a retail company, making a whopping $21 a week. Mom worked for a stockbroker and pulled in an additional $12 per week. In 1941, my dad joined the army and went off to war. He was in the 34th Infantry Division and landed in North Africa. After the campaign in North Africa, his unit was assigned to go to Italy. He landed at Anzio Beach and walked and fought his way the entire length of Italy. Sergeant Bucky Walters won two Purple Hearts and had his right knee torn up badly by shrapnel from a hand grenade. He told me his goal, in addition to staying alive during the war, was to learn five Italian words each day and he succeeded in doing both. By the time he reached the Swiss border he could speak fluent Italian. He also learned to cuss in seven different languages.

Dad was discharged in 1945 and in December of 1946, my sister Barbara was born. I arrived in September of 1949. Dad then began working for the federal government, with his first job being in the post office. He worked hard, was honest, and later became a special investigator for the Social Security Administration. He investigated doctors, drug stores, and hospitals for fraud. If any irregularities or shady deals were apparent, he sent reports to the Federal Bureau of Investigation (FBI). There were numerous bribery attempts and he always said that he could have been a very rich man if he had wanted to be, because he was offered all kinds of illegal incentives to get rid of his information. He wasn't interested. My dad had been in a commando outfit in World War II and he said he learned that the two worst things you could be were a liar and a thief. If he didn't earn it, he didn't want it. He would often say, "Life is no good without principles."

My dad was one month shy of his 60th birthday and about to retire when I was injured. He and Mom had just purchased a new condo at the Covered Bridge retirement community in Freehold, New Jersey. They were all set to relax, travel, and enjoy themselves. They just took those dreams and threw them away. They did it all for me. Mom understood this and was with my dad all the way. As happens a lot of times, the moms stay home and get little of the credit that they deserve. This was certainly true in our case too, but my mom's role was invaluable. She always gave me total love and support in all that I did and any success that I have had is directly linked to her. She was the best.

Dad was a man of many homilies. He was continually making statements such as, "I'm stupid. I don't know how to spell *can't.*" Another one of his favorites was, "If you put enough into it, if you want it to work out, somehow it will." The one that I liked the best, and probably heard the most often, went like this: "If you throw enough shit against the wall, some of it is bound to stick and you will eventually cover the wall." Dad was tireless, optimistic, and persistent in everything he did. He's the one who taught me that if you are going to do something, do it right. He was the driving force behind "The Dennis Walters Golf Show." In the beginning, despite being repeatedly turned down, he made hundreds of calls to golf clubs trying to schedule performances for me. Every once in awhile he would succeed in talking someone into hiring us for $200 a show. Every time this happened it was a major boost to both of us. Dad wore many hats, including those of road manager, equipment manager, and chauffeur. He even helped me care for my dogs. Every night that we were on the road, he followed the same procedure. We would find a motel and he would go in and check it out. We always wanted a quiet room so he would ask for one on the side opposite the highway, not near an elevator, ice machine, or laundry. Naturally, it would take him several tries to satisfy those requirements and I grew used to the fact that it normally took him 30 minutes to check in. We almost always did sleep in a quiet room so it was worth it. Every night he also had to lug in the big golf bag, suitcase, and anything else we needed. In the earlier years, this also included smuggling the dog into some of the fanciest, as well as the more modest, hotels and motels across America.

Into his 80s and with his triple bypass behind him, Dad was slowing down a bit and finally stopped traveling with me. However, he didn't stop helping others. My sister signed him up to be a volunteer at the local elementary school. He was assigned to help the kids who were having problems with reading and math and immediately became known as Grandpa Bucky to everyone in the school. Even today, we still run into the staff from Silver Ridge Elementary School and they always tell us how much they enjoyed the time Dad brought my show dog, Benji Hogan, and me to the school for show-and-tell.

My injury was incredibly traumatic for my parents. In my high school and college years Dad had helped provide me with the opportunities to reach my dreams of the PGA Tour. After the accident, on numerous occasions I can remember him saying to me that if it were possible, he would gladly trade places with me. I am sure in those early years my folks kept thinking, 'He's getting better, he's getting better.' But I wasn't. It would have been easy to panic, to wonder how in the world they could handle it. They stuck together and I think that that was their secret. Fortunately, at the time of my accident, their home in Covered Bridge was just in the process of being built and the contractor was nice enough to make wider doorways and ramps to make things easier for me. The whole thing, though, was not easy for my parents. They had to lift me, help get me to rehab, and do many other things that required a great deal of exertion. One of the hardest things for me to endure, after having lived on my own, was to realize that I needed my parents to help bathe and dress me again. One cannot describe what it is like to lose your sense of dignity. For the next several years, we continued to live in New Jersey before finally making the move to Florida in 1977.

I have been fortunate to have three incredible people in my family who changed their lives for me. I never could have done this by myself. For anyone to do what my dad, my mom, and my sister Barbara did, even if they were family, was a very special thing. How do you adequately thank people for dramatically changing their lives for you? I wish I knew.

I put a lot of effort into the golf show, although I can honestly say it never seems to be work or like a job. I raised a few blisters on my hands, along with blood, sweat, tears and more, but I never could have done this without those three. First of all, when I was in the hospital, my parents drove two hours up and two hours back every single day from Freehold, New Jersey to the hospital in Morristown. Barbara drove nearly the same distance from Shark River Hills. Once I was transferred to Kessler Institute, the drive was cut nearly in half for everyone. It took a lot of energy and per-severance for them to do that. I didn't know at the time that my injury would be permanent, but they knew it from the beginning. As the truth began to sink in for me, my frustration continued to grow. It had to be hard for them to see me like that. Once, I had a promising golf career in front of me and then I was without the use of my legs for the rest of my life. I didn't really know what I was going to do or how I would handle what fate had handed me. Months later, I simply blew up one day and lost my cool. I took my fist and punched a hole right through the wall of my parents' brand-new condo. Luckily, I did no severe damage to my fist, although at the time it would not have mattered to me. I had no idea how I was going to cope with this over the long haul. I had no idea what my parents were thinking, but I knew it was killing them.

During my recovery when I was trying to give it my 100% ef-fort, Dad was just unbelievable. I was trying to improve and get better. I kept thinking, "Isn't that what golf is all about? Isn't that what life is all about?" It's all about trying to be the best you can be. The worst, and perhaps easiest, thing you can do is give up. My parents, especially Dad, wouldn't let me give up. He had this poem he used to recite. It went this way:

It's simple and easy to laugh and sing
when life goes along like a song.
But the man worthwhile is the man who can smile
when everything goes dead wrong.

For me, everything did go dead wrong, and it really was hard to smile. But I just kept going because I had the desire and support I needed. I can only judge through my own eyes, but I feel that whatever the bottom is, I have been there. I lived there for a long time. In my case, as depressed as I was, I never once considered seeing a psychiatrist because I knew what my problem was. I was 24 years old and no longer had the use of my legs. I mean, golf was everything and in one moment of time, it had been taken away from me. There was no way my life would ever be the same. It's not like a cold, the flu, or a virus. Those will always go away. This, the paralysis, was there to stay. Just because I was able to hit a golf ball again didn't mean that my depression was over. Depression was something I had to fight then and it still continues to haunt me at times even now.

The questions that seemed to bother me most were how would I cope with my situation and how could I find a way out of the dark hole that I was in? Simply knowing that you're never going to get any better was enough to cause the deepest of depressions. Many people get depressed about things, but usually there are cures or medication that will make them better. That was not the case with me. One thing that you almost have to create is an alter ego. You have to almost think that you are two people and all the bad things are happening to this other guy and not to you. I think if there is an obstacle in your path, you have to find a way to either go over it, around it, or cope with it. That's what life is all about. In my case, the medicine was golf. For someone else, anything positive—such as music, reading, writing, painting, whatever—could be their medicine. That's what I tell people. If you have the desire, you can find the answer.

My family has enabled me to learn a lot of lessons and I believe we understand sacrifice better than many. I think many people don't realize that you can learn something from the bad things that happen to you. You are going to be better and you are going to improve because of the bad times. Problems and obstacles should not always be looked upon as negatives. They can be opportunities to show how good you are and how good you can be. The other part of the equation is desire. You can't teach desire. It is something you have to have inside of you. I think that if you have desire you can achieve almost anything. People today are too quick to have an excuse for their shortcomings. Admittedly, I struggled with overwhelming obstacles immediately after the accident. My first goal was simply survival, trying to find a reason to go on. There was a sense of total bewilderment about what had happened. It doesn't really sink in at first. You don't want to accept the cold hard facts of the truth. After being independent, traveling overseas, living the life that I had so passionately pursued—all of that was snuffed out that day on the cart path. Where I once took care of everything, I was then totally dependent on others to do things for me. It destroys your self-image. You lose all sense of human dignity. This was something that I did not overcome quickly. It literally took me years to feel decent again about myself. To this day, I still get depressed because I'm never going to be the way I was. If nothing else, I've learned the benefits of having a strong will and the desire to succeed. I have tried to show others, by my own personal example, that it is always possible to follow your dreams. I just happened to choose golf.

There are so many different ways to overcome the challenges of life and what it throws at you. I hope other people will see what I did and take encouragement from that. If there is something you really want to do, no matter how impossible it may seem, if you are willing to work hard and persevere, you can achieve success at almost anything. When you actually think about it, there are very few things that are impossible. I always close my golf show with that message, hoping to give my audience motivation and inspiration to follow their dreams. I hope people who hear about my story will gain some positive thought from my example, or if not from me, then from whatever source that can help them. I think, again, it all starts with the desire to improve. If you have a little of that, you will surely be encouraged to continue your fight and your situation is bound to get better. My family helped me understand all of this and I love them so much for it.

My parents were both unbelievable in their assistance and support to me, but there is the third person, my sister Barbara, who is one of the most extraordinary persons I know. Suffice it to say that we went through all the normal sibling rivalries and confrontations that are part of growing up. At the time of my accident, Barbara was a physical education teacher in Tinton Falls, New Jersey, and really loved her job. While I was in the hospital and at Kessler Institute during my rehabilitation, she taught school until 3 o'clock every afternoon and then got in the car and drove to see me nearly every day. After I came home to the condo, her travel time was reduced considerably, but she still showed up on a daily basis. When we finally moved to Florida, these visits only occurred during school holidays. In 1987, she decided to apply for a school sabbatical and pursue her master's degree. She chose to go to school in Florida so that at least for the year, she would be near us again. It was great having Barbara and her daughter, Brodie, around. Mom and Dad loved the fact that they could spend time with their only granddaughter. During that year, when she was not studying, Barbara, as always, pitched in to help me. The "Dennis Walters Golf Show" was still in the developmental stage and we were struggling with things. Dad was really against computers and this made all the paperwork involved with my show a nightmare. He did not trust computers and used the hunt-and-peck method to type out individually all of my show contracts. He printed my schedule on a legal pad and every time we added a show, he would have to start all over again on a clean sheet of paper. This was not the first time Dad expressed his opinion about some damn new invention that was going nowhere. Air-conditioning also fell into this category. In the late 1950s, against all of his protests, and much to Barbara's and my relief, Mom went out to Sears and bought a small window air-conditioner unit for the family room. After all that fuss, guess who was always parked on the couch enjoying the cool room? That's right, dear old Dad.

I convinced Barbara to stay in Florida for another year, because it seemed as though things always ran better when she was around. She took "The Dennis Walters Golf Show," into the computer age and had us organized in no time. Unlike my parents, who tended to coddle me, she pushed me. I always figured that conducting the shows and hitting golf balls was my part of the deal. It was pretty clear from the beginning that Barbara had other ideas. While I was content to be the golfer and my dad the gofer, Barbara would have no part of that. For the first couple of years her main responsibility was handling the mounds of paperwork that had increased on a daily basis as my show began to grow. However, when Dad fell in Memphis in August of 1994 and broke his arm in three places, Barbara was called into action as a temporary replacement. Barbara and I struggled with things that never before had been a problem for me when I was with Dad. For example, when I drove to a show, I would always pull my golf cart on a trailer behind our minivan. However, when I had to fly to a show, I needed to take my portable seat and then assemble it on a golf cart at the course where I was doing the show. It took my dad half an hour to set up the seat and get things ready for me to hit balls, but it would take Barbara and me two hours, because neither of us was adept at engineering functions. We realized how much we had to learn and also understood what an important part Dad had played in the show. It took us a while but we finally got the hang of things and eventually found our own routine.

As I mentioned, Dad did everything when we were on the road. With Barbara, things were different and my life was about to change again. She thought it only fair that we work on a 50-50 basis, and for me this was a totally new concept. And when she said 50-50, she meant it. When she drove her two hours, no matter where we were, she pulled over and said it was my turn. When I traveled with Dad, he did 90% of the driving and I did the other 10%. In the past, I always went into the clubhouse and talked to all the guys while Dad set up the seat and made all the arrangements. Not so with Barbara. I was now put in charge of the mechanics of putting the seat together, and as a result I can now get it ready in about 15 minutes. Because of Barbara I became better and tougher and was able to hold my own in any situation.

After that first summer on the road with me, Barbara spent the next few years going with me whenever Dad wanted to take a break. She found being on the road all the time tough, especially when she had to carry that heavy golf bag into the hotel room every night, and she really missed being at home with Brodie, who was 12 at the time. Brodie stayed with her dad or her grandmother, but always was going back and forth, which was difficult for her. Eventually we started traveling in a motor home, and that made things a lot better. Motor-home living is great because you have all the conveniences of home while you are on the road. For the last four years I have been lucky enough to represent Newmar Motor Homes on my tour. They provide me with a fabulous and comfortable 40-foot Mountain-Aire that makes my life so much easier.

Barbara did a great job on the road for five years, but she really prefers staying at home and handling the business part of my show. I got used to traveling with her and things were working well, but again I found myself looking for my third assistant. It seems as if I just keep wearing them out. I have hired a college student for the last four summers to travel with me and be my assistant and it has worked out well. Barbara supports me so much and is fond of saying to people, "He's not handicapped, he just can't walk." She also says "Sure he has bad days, but everybody has bad days. He's not having a bad day because he's handicapped, he's having a bad day because he's having a bad day." Both my sister and I have grown a lot in the last 27 years. She has been an enormous source of strength to me, and without her contributions I would not be where I am today. As I look back on things, I often tell Barbara, "For better or worse, we have stuck together. We are a family. That is our strength." Is everything perfect? Of course not, but we don't pretend that it is. Like it or not, we deal with whatever it is we have to deal with and continue on from there.

— *Chapter 26* —

Still Showing Off

I'M PROUD TO SAY that my golf show has succeeded far beyond any expectations I may have had at the beginning of my career. To be honest, when I started I never actually thought I could make a career out of being a golf performer. Mostly what I was doing, I'm sure, was attempting to escape the reality of my situation and, in the process, get a little exercise. Obviously, I hated not being able to walk and play golf and compete in tournaments. But when I began to do my show, I noticed that I actually enjoyed performing for people and that the endeavor did a lot to fill the void that I'd been left with. That's when I knew that I wanted to pursue doing my golf show as a way of making a living. Today, I'm very proud of the fact that my livelihood, to a large extent, depends on my ability to hit a golf ball well. This gives each and every shot that I hit meaning, and it spurs me on to always try to improve. It was always my dream to go on tour, but I never envisioned it to be like this. However, in a way far different than what I imagined, I have achieved my lifelong personal goal. I am a professional golfer.

Something else I'm very pleased about is the business side of my life. I have 15 wonderful sponsors—Arizona Beverages, Boca Resorts, Continental Airlines, The Golf Channel, Guess Watches, Jelly Belly Candy Company, Jersey Mike's Subs, Newmar Motor Homes, Nike Golf, Orlimar, Sprint, UST Graphite Shafts, Winn

Grips, and the Yamaha Golf Car Company—and I represent these companies proudly on my tour. Benji Hogan is proud to have a sponsor, too: the IAMS Company, manufacturers of Eukenuba dog food.

In addition to the great business relationship that we have with these companies, we have a great personal relationship. I truly believe in loyalty, but also believe that it is a two-way street. My sponsors support me 100% and I give 100% back—and not just on the days when I do my show, but 365 days a year.

With that said, I'm now about to enter an exciting new phase of my career as I begin a working relationship with the United States Golf Association Foundation. As of January 2002, the USGA Foundation has become one of my show supporters. It is a first for the organization in its 107-year history. The USGA, of which the foundation is its charitable arm, writes the rules of golf which we all play by. They conduct 13 national championships and their Foundation and Resource Center helps to grow the game for everyone. This new association with the USGA Foundation is one of the highest honors I have ever had and I'm confident that it will help me spread my message of inspiration and hope to a much wider audience. My thanks to former USGA Presidents Trey Holland and Judy Bell and Executive Director David Fay for their faith in me. As I have done in the past, it will be my mission to reach out to as many people as I can to show them the beauty and joy that the game of golf has to offer. To be able to do this in conjunction with the USGA Foundation is a wonderful, historic opportunity.

Each year, I make approximately 100 appearances all over the United States and Canada. I drive to about two-thirds of these shows in a Newmar Mountain-Aire Motor Home. Newmar has been a sponsor of my show for the past four years. For me, traveling in a motor home is the absolute best. Seven years ago, my sister said that if she was going to travel with me and help with the show, a motor home was the only way to go. It provides all the comforts of home and it eliminates the two worst things about traveling: eating out in restaurants and staying in a different hotel every night. Back then, even before Newmar became a sponsor, we decided that their motor homes were the best on the market. We bought our first Newmar in Phoenix, Arizona, in 1994. On our drive home to Florida, I knew that Barbara, as usual, had come up with a winning idea. On that trip home, we stopped at a rest area near Van Horn, Texas, the town where Ben Hogan had his near-fatal car accident in 1949. It was the Saturday of the Masters, and as we watched the tournament on our satellite dish—eating sandwiches, drinking lemonade, and munching on popcorn—I knew that I was really going to like this new way of traveling. There we were, out in the middle of nowhere, watching golf on television. One of the items we have added to our travel equipment is a trailer that carries my golf cart behind the motor home. It makes it so much easier to have my own specialized golf cart.

When you see me at a show and I'm using a red golf cart, the chances are very good that I drove to that show. If I have to fly to an event, I bring my portable seat and attach it to a cart that's always provided by a local Yamaha dealer. More often than not, that golf cart will be cream in color.

My routine on show day is pretty much standard. I arrive about two hours early and begin to set up for my performance. This process starts with finding a good spot to do the show. Most shows are conducted either on the driving range or on a tee box that is close to the clubhouse. Once the location has been determined, I pick a spot where the gallery will have the best view and I line my cart up properly. Barbara or one of my other assistants begins to arrange the needed props and we test the sound system. I also like to hit some warm-up shots before the audience starts to arrive. Another thing is making sure that Benji Hogan is comfortable and safe. An extra cart that we borrow from the host pro serves two purposes. It provides shade for Hogan, and it's a good place to hang our sponsor banner.

When all of this is done, we're ready to begin the show. After the host professional makes the introduction, we usually have a question and answer period. I added this segment to my show about a dozen years ago and it was one of the best ideas I ever had. It's a great way for me to get to know the audience and for them to get to know me. Quite often the questions are about swing tips and the type of equipment that I use. I also incorporate my story into these sessions. Anyone who asks a question gets one of my logoed golf balls with a beautiful picture of Benji Hogan on it. It's a great way to set the tone for the rest of the show.

I continue with a brief introduction about my program and then I prepare them for one of the strongest opening acts in show business: Benji Hogan. After he is introduced, Benji will run out and jump on his special chair, which has been set up alongside my golf cart. He starts out by waving to the crowd and then he gives me a high five. We next do our bit with the box of tissues that I've already told you about, and then move on to my asking him questions, with him barking out the answers. About three or four people from the crowd ask him questions to conclude his performance, which lasts about 10 minutes. It is, without any doubt, a crowd pleaser.

When Benji's finished, it's time for me to go to work. I start my show by hitting a ball that Hogan has already teed up for me and then hit a few more warm-up shots. While I'm doing this, I explain to the audience what I feel are the benefits and joys of the game. I conclude this portion of the show by stressing that the most important aspect of golf is that it can be very enjoyable. Then it's on to the FUN part of the show.

In my hour-long show, I usually hit about 25 trick shots (or as I call them, "shots from unusual lies"). Each shot has a story that I tell to the audience while my assistant gets everything ready. The shot itself is usually the punch line for the story. Near perfect coordination between my assistant and me is vital so that there isn't any dead time between each shot. The hour contains plenty of humor and a lot of audience participation. I like to describe my show as "great golf, great fun, and a great message."

In order for me to do a successful show, I have to do a lot of practicing. If Barbara isn't available to help, my good friend Danny Eccleston is always willing to lend a hand. In fact, Danny knows my routine almost as well as I do and has assisted me many times. Danny is from England and is a well-known gaffer in the film industry. He likes to tell the crowd that he is my English butler. It always gets a laugh.

A good drive for me is about 230 yards, but I still hit it far enough to impress the audience. What I'm most proud of is my accuracy. I can hit every one of my trick shots with the same little right-to-left draw and when I'm finished I have made it easy for the range picker to gather the balls because they are all in the same small area. This gives me enormous satisfaction.

The clubs that I use to do some of my trick shots are made out of unusual items. I have a club made from a fishing rod, one made from an old crutch, one that's an actual radiator hose, and another made from a cell phone. I hit a shot with a club that has three heads and one that has three universal joints in the shaft. I hit a golf ball off a watch and one of my shots involves balancing an egg on a ball and then hitting the ball but not breaking the egg. I hit balls off tees that are up to three feet high. I also demonstrate how I putt by getting up on my crutches, balancing on one crutch, and putting the ball one-handed. I have had great success putting this way. One time I was in Utah and the participants in the tournament were involved in a putting contest. Everyone drew numbers to determine the order of participation and, naturally, I drew number one. The putt we were all going to try to make was from the far side of the green, a 60-footer. I hiked across the green on my crutches, lined up my putt, and stroked it dead center into the hole. No one else even came close.

After I demonstrate how I putt, I show the art of "long putting" by hitting a shot 200 yards using my putter. My semifinal shot in the show consists of hitting a drive through fire. The trick that seems to be the favorite of most audiences, though, is the last one in my show. I call it the "Machine-Gun Shot" because I hit ball after ball in rapid-fire as they're rolled down a ramp in front of me. That final trick never fails to draw oohs and aahs from the audience.

The shots that I do are intended to show that if someone has a good swing, they can hit a golf ball well with almost anything. *Off* almost anything, too. When I hit a ball off the top of an Arizona Ice Tea can, I always joke that it is the best "tee" I have ever used. As a way of thanking the spectators for attending my show, I always give away some of my props. Someone will get the Arizona Ice Tea, an adult will get a Guess Watch, a junior will get a Jelly Belly Watch, and everyone will get a package of Jelly Belly candy. We used to give out the Jelly Bellies at the beginning of the show, but found that Benji Hogan was too distracted to concentrate on his opening act. All he could think about was getting some of the candy. Now we wait until his performance is over before we hand out the candy.

Being a performer (and something of a ham), no crowd is too small. However, I most enjoy a group of 250 to 300 people. I also like to have them as close to me as possible because it makes them feel as if they're a part of the show. Plus, it's easier for me to interact with them. The smallest crowd I ever performed for consisted of 11 people. My biggest crowd was 33,000 at Anaheim Stadium in California. The size of the crowd doesn't matter to me; I always give it my best.

My show concludes with a thank-you to my sponsors and the host professional and, of course, to the audience because they are the ones who make my performances possible. Just before I hit my last shot, I remind the audience of the lesson that I learned many years ago when I was told that it would be impossible for me to ever play golf again. I suggest that perhaps there is something in their lives that seems impossible to attain. I then encourage them to remember that with hard work and perseverance, they can be successful at almost anything.

*   *   *

Over the years, I have been fortunate to receive several high honors. In addition to the 1977 Ben Hogan Award, I was presented with an honorary lifetime membership in the PGA of America. Only six other individuals—former President Gerald R. Ford, Bob Hope, Gary Player, attorney Lloyd Lambert, former PGA advisory committee member John Jachym, and Dr. Trey Holland, president of the USGA in 2000 and 2001—have been granted this honor. In 1994, the National Golf Foundation presented me with their highest honor—The Graffis Award—for contributions to the game. I was also recently inducted into the University of North Texas Hall of Fame. On top of that, the International Network of Golf presents an annual Dennis Walters Award. I'm happy that my friend John Nicholas is the latest recipient.

When *Golfweek* magazine inaugurated its Father of the Year award in 1983, I'm proud to say that my father, Bucky Walters, was the first recipient.

*   *   *

I have written this book with the hope that my story and my own experiences in trying to achieve a seemingly impossible dream will inspire others to pursue their dreams as I have chased mine. It is not an easy thing to do, and sometimes the road to dreamsville is full of potholes and obstacles. The key to success, however, is to find a way over . . . around . . . or through those obstacles. And to persevere as I have done.

Keep dreaming and keep trying. You can do it, too.

– Epilogue –

A Word or Two from Barbara

FOR YEARS, I HAD TOLD DENNIS that he should turn his story into a book and share it with the rest of the world. He always agreed with me, but he always asked the same question, too: "Who would buy it?"

It was my thinking that, deep down, he was afraid of proposing the book idea to a publisher, only to have it rejected. Thanks to Brian and Anne Lewis of Sleeping Bear Press, who approached *us* with a book idea in the lobby of the Peabody Hotel in Orlando during the 1999 PGA Merchandise Show, Dennis didn't have to face rejection. He'd had enough of that already in his life.

In the past when Dennis and I jokingly talked about writing a book, we fantasized about which Hollywood stars would portray us when the book was turned into a big screen blockbuster. We really never did decide who should play us in the movie, but we were in total agreement that the actor Carroll O'Connor would have been perfect in the role of our dad. Unfortunately, both of these fine men passed away before this book could be published. Much like "Archie Bunker," our dad was a real character and a creature of habit. Each morning after he got dressed, he would pick up a stack of Dennis's golf show brochures and put them in his back pocket. Everywhere he went he would hand one out and say, "That's my son." After our dad passed away, I went to the hospital to collect his personal items. In the nightstand in his room, I found a stack of Dennis's brochures. Up to the end, he was still his son's biggest fan.

After I began to help Dennis with his book, I learned a lot about my brother that I never knew or realized. Clearly, Dennis and Jim Achenbach had put their hearts and souls into making this a book that would be memorable and meaningful to everyone who read it. My brother is a man of few words when it comes to emotion, so I know that putting his feelings down on paper was one of the most difficult things he has ever done. When we finished each chapter, Dennis and I would sit side-by-side at the computer to reread it and make corrections. Certain sections had us holding back tears, others had us laughing out loud. Remembering incidents that we had not thought about in years was very cathartic for us.

The past year has been difficult for Dennis and me; we lost both of our parents. Even though we have always been close, I think 2001 brought Dennis and me even closer. Oh, we still fight and get mad at each other, like a brother and sister will do. And sometimes I'll blurt out, "I can't wait to get my own life!" But when it comes right down to it, my brother and I are stuck with each other. And do you know what? I wouldn't have it any other way.

I'm prejudiced, of course, but I feel that Dennis personifies a true professional athlete, and I only wish that more people would give him the respect that I feel he so richly deserves. He has earned it, not only through his contributions to the game of golf, but through his contributions to society as well. I get angry sometimes when he'll make a dozen phone calls a day, leaves messages, and not even get a single call returned. I see the hurt in his eyes, and I'm sure he feels—though he rarely verbalizes it—that he's being ignored because of his disability.

One year at the PGA Merchandise Show, Dennis was told to stay out of a certain booth because it would make the CEO of the company uncomfortable to have him there. Believe me, one of these days that CEO and I are going to have a little chat. When we do, I can guarantee it that he will not have a problem understanding everything I have to say. And if he thought my brother made him uncomfortable, well . . . just wait until Dennis's big sister gets hold of him.

I truly hope that you have enjoyed this book and have gained something from sharing the joys and sorrows of Dennis's life. I would also like to invite you to attend one of his shows. It's an experience that will make you feel good about life. I often tell Dennis that the way he sees the world today is much different than how he would have seen it if he had retained the use of his legs. I also have no doubt that he would have been a huge success on the PGA Tour, and now would be a top draw on the PGA Senior Tour. Dennis, unfortunately, had to find his own tour, but it's a tour that I feel makes him the biggest star of all.

And if you want to know that dreams really do come true, he's all the proof you need.

Barbara Walters Herman
Plantation, Florida

– *Acknowledgments* –

I WOULD LIKE TO take the opportunity to thank some people who were very instrumental in helping me achieve success and my dreams, and to also thank those folks who contributed to the writing of this book. My sister Barbara fits both categories. She has helped me my entire life and was brilliant in the contributions she made to this book. Everyone should have a sister like her. I am very sad that my mom and dad both passed away before the book was published because they were looking forward to seeing it in print. It is gratifying to me that they knew I was able to overcome unprecedented odds and accomplished my dream of becoming a successful professional golfer. They made tremendous sacrifices for me and I could not have asked for better parents. I also want to thank my niece Brodie and her new husband, Daniel, for their love and support. It goes without saying how much I appreciate my friends Gary Wiren and Wayne Warms for their lifetime friendships. Danny Eccelston has been one of my best friends for my adult life and it is a comfort to know that I can always count on him. It was Danny who suggested the title of the book, and I can honestly say it captures the essence of what you read. This book would not have been possible without the help of my talented friend and writer Jim Achenbach, who coauthored this book. His countless hours of research and interviews have made the details of this book possible. In many cases he drew things out of me that I had long ago forgotten and thought I wanted to forget.

Thanks to Brian and Anne Lewis of Sleeping Bear Press, who believed I had a good story to tell and to my editor, Brett Marshall, for his guidance and encouragement that helped to make this book a reality. I also want to thank Danny Freels for his efforts in fine-tuning the manuscript and making all my words and thoughts sound right. And thanks to all the others at Sleeping Bear Press who contributed to the editing and design of the book. Writing this book was not an easy task but I feel that I gave it my all. That was the one objective that I had when we undertook this project, and I feel that we have succeeded.

Thanks to all of my sponsors who believe in me and my program, and for making it possible for "The Dennis Walters Golf Show" to reach as many people as I have in the past and will continue to do so in the future. It takes a lot of help and support to do 100 shows a year, and I am grateful to all the companies that I work with. I wish to express my appreciation to noted golf instructor David Leadbetter, a good friend, for taking the time to analyze my swing—maybe now I will hit the ball even better! I am looking forward with great excitement to my historic new relationship with the United States Golf Association Foundation and to working with them to grow the game of golf, especially for those individuals with physical disabilities to overcome.

Finally, I can't do the acknowledgments without thanking the hundreds of thousands of people who have viewed my show and have made me feel like a welcomed guest at all their events. Good luck, good golf, and I hope our paths cross soon.